I0141905

Start with Your Results in Mind

Whatever you do, start your plan early, update it, refine it, and think about it always. Your success depends on what you think about the most.

Life Stages Lessons
Salvation, Stewardship,
Wellness, Works

Aging Reading Certification Series
Volume 5
Second Edition

Robert W. Chism, CAM

Copyright © 2014 Robert W. Chism
All Rights Reserved
ISBN: 978-0986190148
Date March 21, 2015

Published by New Beginnings
www.gonewbeginnings.com/
C/O Robert W. Chism (Bob)
2403 Carmen Court
Lindhurst, IL 60046
chism.w.robert@comcast.net
847-395-1626

The most appropriate categories for this book are religious aging leadership and self-help aging.

Reiteration has been used as a teaching method to reinforce ideas and theory in all my books.

Neither New Beginnings nor this book supports any one political party over another or advocates any one religion over another. It does promote change based upon an added longevity bonus of 30 years, the new elderhood life stage, young and old ageism amelioration, intergenerational understanding as well as generation and life stage cognizance.

The book was written as a seminary text for training and equipping students; for seminary, graduate pastors; and elderhood protirement non-specialists desiring an education for the best use their time for the Lord.

The book is a volume for an Aging Reading Certification Series and any age in planning their legacy life.

All New Beginnings book royalties, after expenses, are contributed to funding research and free services.

Table of Contents

Aging Resources

Prologue

The Bill of Rights

America was founded on the principle that every person has God-given rights; power belongs to the people, and the government exists to protect our rights.

The Escape of the Courageous Pilgrims

The Pilgrims were English Separatists who founded Plymouth Colony in 1620. The Pilgrims, fleeing religious persecution, broke away from the Church of England because they felt the Church violated biblical principles of true Christians. Due to abuse and economic distress, they believed they had to break away from the Church of England to form congregations that were more in keeping with divine requirements. The Church was under the strict rule of the State, so their actions were considered treasonous, and these Separatists had to flee their homeland. Determined and very courageous men and women committed themselves (in all aspects of their lives) to a life based on the Bible and a relationship with God. They brought their only known culture and spiritual values to the New World and attempted to establish an improved foundation of English society on an unfamiliar new continent. For Pilgrims, it was a matter of survival.

Source: http://www.allabouthistory.org/pilgrims.htm

America Religious Refugees

Many of the British North American colonies that eventually formed the United

States of America were settled in the 17th Century by men and women, who, in the face of European persecution, refused to compromise passionately held religious convictions and fled Europe. The New England colonies, New Jersey, Pennsylvania, and Maryland were conceived and established "as plantations of religion." Some settlers who arrived in these areas came for secular motives--"to catch fish," as one New Englander put it--but the great majority left Europe to worship God in the way they believed to be correct. They enthusiastically supported the efforts of their leaders to create "a city on a hill" or a "holy experiment," whose success would prove that God's plan for His churches could be successfully realized in the American wilderness. Even colonies like Virginia, which were planned as commercial ventures, were led by entrepreneurs who considered themselves "militant Protestants" and worked diligently to promote the prosperity of the church.

Source:www.loc.gov/exhibits/religion/rel01.html

The Right to Vote

We the people have the right to vote for change, change that will restore and preserve our inalienable rights as instituted by our Founding Fathers and guaranteed in the documents they gave us as a free people.

Declaration of Independence

We hold these truths to be self-evident, that all men are created equal, that they are endowed by their Creator with certain unalienable Rights, that among these are Life,

Liberty and the pursuit of Happiness.--That to secure these rights, Governments are instituted among Men, deriving their just powers from the consent of the governed, -- That whenever any form of Government becomes destructive of these ends, it is the Right of the People to alter or to abolish it, and to institute new Government, laying its foundation on such principles and organizing its powers in such form, as to them shall seem most likely to affect their Safety and Happiness.

Amendment I to U.S. Constitution

Congress shall make no law respecting an establishment of religion, or prohibiting the free exercise thereof; or abridging the freedom of speech, or of the press, or the right of the people peaceably to assemble and to petition the Government for a redress of grievances.

We the people have the right to vote for change; change that will restore and preserve our inalienable rights as instituted by our Founding Fathers and guaranteed in the documents they gave us as a free people.

The Four Freedoms

The Four Freedoms described in President Franklin D. Roosevelt's historic January 6, 1941 State of the Union address, freedom of speech and expression, freedom of religion, freedom from want, and freedom from fear became a rallying point for the United States during WWII. Artist Norman Rockwell created four vignettes to illustrate the concepts. The Saturday Evening Post first published them in

February and March 1943. Popular reaction was overwhelming, and more than 25,000 readers requested full-color reproductions suitable for framing. Subsequently, they were used by the War Department to sell bonds for the war effort.

This book is devoted to life stages lessons to prepare elderhood adults better to implement protirement service opportunities, as well as devote themselves to participatory democracy and protecting the homeland against government unconstitutionally.

Introduction

Due to longevity, traditional human life stages have become outdated. The new life stages are as follows:

Emerging Adults (20-34)

Full Adults (Late 30s

Sandwich Generation Adults (40s-Mid 60s)

Elderhood Adults (65-84)

Frail Adults (85 plus)

Since graduating from the public sector, there has time to write articles, books, and guides on the second half of life

In his book, *The Third Age*, Dr. William Sadler defines a new life course. The following chart outlines each age having twenty to twenty-five years in a given life span, stage and the particular focus:

Age	Stage	Focus
0-25	Preparation	The first age is a time of growing up.
26-50	Achievement	The second age is a time of establishment.
51-75	Fulfillment	The third age is the time of a more caring life.
76-up	Completion	The fourth age is a time of integration. *

* Polishing off, coming to terms with life, acceptance of eternity.

The third and fourth ages are where second-halfers will spend the rest of their lives. According to Nancy Cosgriff and Melita

DeBellis, the principals of Third Age Partners and associates of the Center for Third Age Leadership, the third age challenge lies in the response-ability to give back, to find the best way to contribute money, talent, and time to address the needs of community and world. The fourth age is the last stage of earthly life. It allows one to review and revel in the fullness of one's life with no regrets and prepare for eternity. The time is a continuation of awareness and acceptance of our physical mortality and faith of our spiritual life for eternity. It is a time of peace, joy, and surrender to the GREAT I AM. All of life is preparation and a prelude to this stage of life.

Elderhood is a new life stage (sixty-five to eighty-four), the next life step after adulthood. This paradigm shift has occurred due to a combination of events: longevity, better education, greater health awareness, discretionary time, and self-dependence.

Protirement (proh.TYR.munt) *means* retiring or quitting an unattractive job to pursue work or hobbies more suited to one's personality. The fact is that God gave us thirty more years of life for a reason. Longevity permits us to accomplish the following scripture:

The Ten Commandments
Exodus 20:1-17 (NIV)

Trust in God Commandment
Psalms 118.8 (NKJV)

The Sermon on the Mount
Matthew 5-7 (NIV)

The Building of His Church Commission
Matthew 16:18 (NIV)

The Great Commandment
Matthew 22:37-40 (NIV)

The Great Commission
Matthew 28:19-20 (NIV)

The Sermon on the Plain
Luke 6:17-49 (NKJV)

The Longevity Response-Ability
Commission John 3:16 (NIV)

The Stewardship Commandment
Colossians 3:23–24 (NIV)

Rejoice & Give Thanks Commandment
1 Thessalonians 5:16-18

The essential lessons in this book are salvation and stewardship.

The entire family, grandkids, elder mom's & dad's and grandparents can benefit from the book. God made us with a purpose. *Life Stages Lessons* focuses on the matters that make a difference in this life and make all the difference in eternity. For success, early development of a life plan and constant refinement. This Alpha Tau Omega guide-book provides how to make the most of life and eternity.

The book covers life long Financial, Spiritual, Physical, and Mental Health. Elderhood & Protirement is a critical section of preparation that could give a 10-year leg-up for contribution time. I have listed Elderhood Protirement Life Guides and Service. Each chapter begins with a quote or other motivating thought and concludes with key takeaways.

The book has been tremendously enhanced by outstanding pathfinder Milton Crum's *"I'm Frail"* in the Fragility chapter and *"Joe's Story"* by Erica Capri in the Eternity chapter of the book.

The benefit of this book in direct proportion to the time put into reading and re-reading the book. Think about the book and how it could apply to life. Pray about it. Start a study group and hear what others think and are doing to make the most of their second-half for God and nation. Start a plan now, update it, refine it and think about it always.

A life plan should be devoid of pride, envy, wrath, greed, sloth, gluttony and lust according to the Bible.

The life plan should include school, college, family, church, career, life long learning and constitutional government service for a better nation and society. Get involved. It is time to take back America as a Christain nation.

Financial Health Stewardship

"If you will live like no one else, later you can live like no one else," Dave Ramsey.

One of the essential lessons of life is financial responsibility. It is necessary to live within one's means and plan for now and the future. Building wealth is about stewardship, not ownership, Psalm: 24:1 (KJV).

Finance and strategic planning were a part of a 40-year business career. In this chapter, Dave Ramsey and Larry Burke (deceased) illustrative information is quoted. Each man is a Christian and a professional authority on the subject, as well as responsive to one of the nation's most pressing needs: government and individual fiscal responsibility.

God provides a quite clear formula in the Bible for financial peace. The Bible mentions money over 800 times. Very simply wealth building is a Holy activity according to Proverbs 10:4 (NIV). Many believe that everyone's wealth should be equal, but the Bible says otherwise in Matthew 26:6 (NIV).

Over three-quarters of Americans are bankrupted, broke & busted by credit cards. Education for lifetime budgeting and the second half of life plans need to become a religious and government priority.

A budget is a crucial document to financial health. Few people have a budget. Budgets are not accessible because they require discipline, focusing on the necessities, rather than wants and wishes, of life.

1

Nowhere in the Bible does it say being poor is good or growing wealth is wrong. The Bible is clear. All good things are of God. During our lifetime, we are His stewards as to all His gifts. We are merely stewards of what God has entrusted to us. As caretakers, it is vital that we use His assets to their fullest potential during our lifetime for our personal, family, business, and charitable interests.

In this section of the chapter, we will provide the how-to of building a budget. An essential element of making a budget is for each spouse to be a critical member of the team.

There are specific priorities or goals for budgeting. In Dave Ramsey's Financial Peace University (FPU), Dave calls them "Tips for Financial Peace:

Pay cash!

$1,000 in an emergency fund

Pay off all debt with the debt snowball

3-6 months of expenses in savings

Invest 15% of income for protirement

College funding

Pay off the house early

Build wealth and give!

An annual budget is a vital management tool to control spending to predetermined necessities.

Creating a budget requires:

Identification of Current Expenditures

Fixed expenses follow:

Tithes

Federal Income Tax (ignore if taxes deducted)

State Income Tax (ignore if taxes deducted)

Federal Social Security (if deducted, ignore)

Medicare (if deducted, ignore)

Housing (mortgage payment or rent)

Utilities (electric, gas, water, et al.)

Automobile(s) (payments, gas, et al)

Now list the variable expenses, items that vary from month to month, but that still have to pay out each month:

Savings/Investment

Outstanding Debts (if applicable)

Food

Utilities

Insurance (life, health, auto)

Entertainment, Recreation

Clothing

Medical/Dental

Miscellaneous

To accurately determine variable expenses, both husband and wife need to keep an expense diary for 30 days. Each purchase, even small, should be listed.

Evaluate spending by historical guidelines:

Charitable Giving	10-15%
Saving / Investing	5-15
Housing	25-35
Utilities	5-10
Food	5-10
Transportation	10-15
Clothing	2-7
Medical/Health	5-10
Personal	5-10
Recreation	5-10

Source: Dave Ramsey's FPU

Track spending to make sure it stays within The above guidelines.

Use standard paper forms or available budgeting software. Relax and take one step at a time.

One drawback of monitoring spending by computer is that it encourages enthusiastic attention to detail. Start by determining which categories of spending can and should be cut (or expanded), concentrate on those categories and worry less about other aspects of your spending.

Watch out for cash leakage. If withdrawals from the ATM evaporate without explanation, it is time to examine where that cash is going.

Spending beyond established limits is dangerous. Figures show that many households with a total income of $50,000 or less are spending more than they bring in. If so, some severe spending cuts are necessary.

Beware of wants or wishes dressed up as necessities.

Spendable budget is net after all government taxes. For example, the government takes the following:

Federal Income

State Income

Federal Social Security

Medicare

Next is to set aside 10-15% for charitable contributions and 5-10% for savings and investments.

When projecting the amount of money available to live on, do not include dollars questionable of being received, such as year-end bonuses, tax refunds or investment gains.

Traditional income sources follow:

Salary

Interest

Dividends

Rents

Royalties

Other Income (garage sales, gifts)

Establish a budget based on the primary income producer. Apply the other spouse's income to one-time purchases only—vacations, furniture, cars—or to savings or debt reduction. Too many times, the pay is interrupted by illness, health leave absence, or a change in employment location.

A caution on both spouses is working. Be sure the income exceeds the expenses and stress of both partners working.

If total income exceeds total expenses, implement a method of budget control. However, if costs exceed revenue, additional controls are necessary. In that case, to reduce costs, an analysis of each budget area is called for using the above spending guideline.

Beware of spending creep. As annual income climbs from raises, promotions and smart investing, do not start paying for luxuries. It is better to use those income increases as an excuse to save more. "Budget Busters" is the vast potential problem areas that can ruin a budget. Failure to control even one of these problems can result in financial disaster in the home.

Major Budget Busters

DEBT: Credit cards, bank loans, and installment credit have made it possible for families to go deeply into debt. Hints for Debt Elimination:

Pray. Ask the Holy Spirit for help and guidance.

Allow no more debt. Destroy all credit cards.

Establish a payment schedule that includes all creditors.

List all assets to evaluate whether or not to sell for immediate debt reduction.

Contact all creditors, honestly relate the problems, and arrange an equitable solution for repayment.

Use a repayment plan, focusing on the higher interest rates first. The average family can be debt free in three years.

Buy on a cash basis, and sacrifice wants and desires until current.

HOUSE: Typically, this is one of the most significant home budget problems. Many families, motivated by peer pressure or some other pressure, buy homes they cannot afford. It is not necessary for everyone to own a home. The decision to buy or rent should be based on needs and financial ability, rather than on internal or external pressure. Tips on buying a house, interest, and real estate taxes down:

Do not buy if it is not possible to stay put.

Start by shoring up credit.

Aim for an affordable home.

The rule of thumb is to buy housing that runs about two-and-one-half times annual salary. However, use one of many calculators available online to get a better handle on how income, debts, and expenses affect what is affordable.

Save until the usual 20 percent put down is available.

Buy in a district with good schools.

Get professional help.

Choose carefully between points and rate.

Before house hunting, get pre-approved.

Do homework before bidding.

Hire a home inspector with guarantees.

Refinance the mortgage.

Appeal home assessment.

AUTO: Many families will buy new cars they cannot afford and trade in their useable vehicle. Many factors enter here, such as ego, esteem, and maturity. Watch Dave Ramsey's video "Drive Free Cars for Life." On YouTube. The current economy makes the calculations inaccurate, but the concept still has potential.

CLOTHING: Many families in debt sacrifice this area in their budget because of excesses in other areas. Moreover, with prudent planning as well as buying and effort, the family can be clothed neatly without great expense:

Saving enough money to buy without using credit.

Educating family members on the care of clothing

Applying discipline with children to enforce these habits.

Developing skills in making and mending clothing

Learn to utilize resources rather than consume them. How many families have closets full of clothes they no longer wear because they are "out of style"?

Many families with large surplus incomes overspend in the area of clothes. Assess whether it matters that to have all of the latest styles. Purchases should reflect good utility rather than ego. Are clothes buys to satisfy a need or a desire? Hints for Clothing Savings:

Make as many of the clothes as time will allow, if possible.

Make a written list of clothing needs and purchase during "off" season, if possible.

Select outfits that can be mixed and used in multiple combinations.

Frequent discount outlets that carry unmarked name-brand goods.

Shop at authentic factory outlet stores for close-out values of top quality.

Select clothing made of home-washable fabrics

Use coin-operated dry cleaning machines instead of commercial cleaners.

Practice early repair for damaged clothing.

Learn to utilize all clothing fully (especially children's wear).

RECREATION/ENTERTAINMENT/DINING : We are a recreation-oriented country. That is not necessarily bad if put in the proper perspective. However, those who are in debt cannot use creditor's money to entertain themselves. Christians must resist this urge and control recreation and entertainment

9

expenses while in debt. What a terrible witness it is for a Christian who is already in financial bondage to indulge at the expense of others.

Hints for Recreation Savings:

Plan vacations during offseasons, if possible.

Consider a camping vacation to avoid motel and food expenses. (Christian friends can pool the costs of camping items.)

Select vacation areas in the general locale.

To reduce expenses and increase fellowship, consider taking vacation trips with two or more families.

If flying, use the least expensive coach fare, i.e., late night or early morning.

Every believer, whether in debt or not, should seek to reduce entertainment/dining out expenses.

WINDFALL: FORGET IT!

Other regular spending areas follow:

SCHOOL AND CHILDCARE This category must reflect those expenses. All different types must be reduced to provide these funds.

MISCELLANEOUS (variable expenses): FOOD: Many families buy too much food. Others buy too little. Typically, the average American family buys the wrong type of food. The reduction of a family's food bill requires quantity and quality planning.

Hints for Grocery Shopping Savings:

Always use a written list of needs.

Try to conserve gas by buying food for a more extended period and in larger quantities.

Avoid shopping when hungry (especially if you are a "sugarholic"). Use a calculator, if possible, to total purchases.

Reduce or eliminate paper products— paper plates, cups, napkins (use cloth napkins).

Evaluate where to purchase sundry items, such as shampoo, mouthwash (these usually are somewhat cheaper at discount stores).

Avoid processed and sugar-coated cereals. (these are expensive, and most of them have little nutritional value).

Avoid prepared foods, such as frozen dinners, pot pies, cakes. (you are paying for expensive labor that you can provide).

Determine good meat cuts that are available from roasts or shoulders, and have the butcher cut these (buying steaks by the package on sale is fairly inexpensive also).

Try store brand canned products. (these usually are cheaper and just as nutritious).

Avoid products on a seasonal price hike.

Substitute or eliminate.

Shop for advertised specials. (Check store entrance).

Avoid buying non-grocery items in a grocery supermarket except on sale. (these are generally high mark-up items).

When possible, purchase food in bulk quantities from large discount stores; the per-item cost is cheaper. Do not buy from convenience stores except in case of emergency.

Use manufacturer's coupons (cents-off on an item or items) only if you were going to buy the thing and it is cheaper than another brand would be without the coupon.

Walmart offers to match any price lower than theirs.

For baby foods, use regular foods processed in a blender.

Leave the children at home to avoid unnecessary pressure.

Check every item as it is being rung up at the store, and again at home.

INSURANCE: It is unfortunate to see so many families misled in this area. Few people understand insurance, either how much is needed or what kind is necessary.

Insurance should be used as a supplementary provision for the family, not for protection or profit. An insurance plan is not designed for saving money or for retirement.

In our society, insurance can be used as an inexpensive vehicle to provide future family income and thus release funds today for family use and the Lord's work.

MEDICAL/DENTAL: Anticipate these expenses in the budget and set aside funds regularly. Failure to do so could lead to indebtedness. Do not sacrifice family health due to lack of planning; but, at the same time, do not use doctors excessively. Proper prevention is much cheaper than correction.

Avoid any dental bills by teaching children to eat the right foods and clean their teeth properly. The dentist will supply all the information needed on this subject.

Avoid doctor bills can in the same way. Take proper care of the body through diet, rest, and exercise. Abuse the body, and ultimately payment is through illnesses and malfunctions. Many diseases or problems are by neglect, but a great many are.

Do not be hesitant to question doctors and dentists in advance about costs. Also, be self-educated to discern when getting good value for one's money. Most ethical professionals will not take offense at these questions. If they do, that may be a hint to change services.

In the case of prescriptions, shop around. Discover the wide variance in prices from one store to the next. Ask about generic drugs. These are usually much less expensive and are just as effective.

The government health care is new and yet to prove itself as promised.

SCHOOL/CHILD CARE: An ever-increasing segment of our population has expenses for private can include multiple items. Some of the costs occur monthly, and others occur on an as-needed basis (such as appliances).

Performing routine maintenance and repair cuts home expenses. Many people rationalize not doing these things on the basis that time is too valuable. That is nonsense. A part of care and maintenance around the home relates to family life, particularly the training of children. When they see Mom and Dad willing to do some physical labor to help around the house, they will learn good habits. Where will they ever learn the skills of self-sufficiency?

Some men avoid working on home projects because they say they lack the necessary skills. Well, those skills are learned, not gifted. Many good books detail every area of home maintenance. Many of these skills will be necessities rather than choices.

VARIABLE INCOME PLANNING: Families with variable monthly incomes need budgets even more than families on fixed salaries. Many people with fluctuating incomes get trapped into debt because they borrow during lean months and spend what they make during high-income months, rather than repaying what they previously borrowed.

Living on a fluctuating income can be very deceiving—and confusing. Months of high income are not a windfall profit. To properly budget a variable income, conservatively estimate annual salary is likely to be, divide that by 12, and then develop a monthly budget based on that amount. Put income into a savings account and withdraw an average monthly salary from that account each month. This method will allow surplus funds from higher income months to accumulate in the savings account to cover budgeted expenses during months of lower income.

Individuals and families with surplus income in their budgets will have the opportunity to invest for retirement or other long-term goals. Being debt-free also will contribute to this category.

Whatever situation, here are some common ways that people can reduce monthly bills:

ELIMINATE NEEDLESS COSTS: Look first for small savings to end budget problems, because of they are easy to find and take advantage. For example, swear off that mid-afternoon, expensive premium latte. Shop for clothes and household furnishings only during sales. Higher gasoline prices make it a good idea to "bundle" shopping trips. Keep the house warmer in summer and cooler in winter. Take on chores that usually paid someone else to perform, such as mowing the lawn or shoveling snow.

REDUCE LARGE EXPENSES: These recommendations are decidedly more painful. If smoking is a problem, take steps to quit. Never buy season tickets to anything. Trade in the luxury car or sport utility vehicle for something a lot cheaper to buy, fuel and maintain (we did say this was painful).

Here are some other specific areas where many people can find savings:

Bargain Shopping

Pet Food

Interest on Debt

Luxury SUV

Speeding Ticket

Large Tax Refund

Uncollected Rebates

Unused Gym Memberships

Tax Return Tips

Use a software tax return service, such as Intuit. TurboTax and an Audit Defense service, such as Tax-Audit.Com. The cost is about $125 depending on package and including a state return.

The benefits are numerous- including tax expertise, quick returns and never having to deal with the IRS directly.

Savings/Investments

Establish savings in the budget. Otherwise, the use of credit becomes a lifelong necessity and debt a way of life. Savings will allow the purchase of items for cash and shop for the best buys, irrespective of the store. Hints for Savings:

Use a company payroll withdrawal, if possible.

Use an automatic bank withdrawal from the checking account.

When an existing debt is paid off, allocate any extra money toward the next most considerable debt.

When all consumer debt is paid off, then reallocate that money to savings.

Pros and Cons of Different Investments from Dave Ramsey's Financial Peace University

Be sure to complete the first four tips noted above. Begin by doing pre-tax savings—in 401(k), 403(b), TSP, Traditional IRA—and tax-free savings—Roth IRA, Roth 401(k). Invest 15% of income. Invest up to the employer matched amount to 401(k), 403(b), or TSP.

Mutual Funds

Ramsey recommends mutual funds for employer-sponsored retirement savings and IRAs. Divide investments equally between each of these four types of funds: Growth, Growth and Income, Aggressive Growth, and International.

Choose A shares (front-end load) and funds that are at least five years old. They should have a solid track record of acceptable returns within their fund category. If risk tolerance is low, this means a shorter time to keep money invested, put less than 25% in aggressive growth or consider adding a "Balanced" fund to the four types of funds suggested.

Single Stocks

Ramsey does not own individual stocks and does not suggest individual stocks as part of an investment plan.

Single stocks do not consistently generate returns as high as mutual funds do in the long-term. If owning a stock for some reason (company stock, fun, whatever), limit single stocks to no more than 10% of the investment portfolio.

Certificates of Deposit (CDs)

Ramsey recommends CDs only for savings (for a purchase, taxes if you own a business), not for long-term investing because of their low rate of return. Long-term investments must earn a high enough percentage to outpace inflation (3-4% per year) and cover taxes on the gains if not inside a retirement account. Most investors need to average a minimum of 6% per year over time to do these two things.

Bonds

Ramsey does not own any bonds and does not suggest them as part of an investment plan. People mistakenly believe bonds are "safe" investments that have slightly lower rates of return than equities. Single bonds can be very volatile and go down significantly in value. Bond mutual funds can at least be tracked for historical returns but do not offer the returns equity mutual funds do.

Fixed Annuities

Ramsey does not own any fixed annuities and does not suggest them as part of an investment plan. Just stay away from these!

Variable Annuities (VAs)

Variable annuities cause more confusion than any other financial product. What are they? AVA is a savings contract with a life insurance company:

They offer tax-deferred growth on an after-tax investment.

They offer beneficiary designation, which allows account transfer to a beneficiary outside of probate court.

VAs carries penalties for early withdrawal (usually a declining surrender charge that lasts from 6 to 11 years).

10% IRS penalty for withdrawing before age 59 ½.

VAs offer many bells and whistles, such as guarantees of principal, life insurance.

VA fees vary widely.

Ramsey has strong suggestions for investors considering VAs:

Only consider Vas the last alternative, i.e., when debt free, including home—and all other tax-deferred options used.

Vas can be useful investment tools because they allow investments to grow tax-deferred.

When purchasing VAs, understand the fees, surrender period, and any riders or options chosen.

When purchasing VAs, stay with the four types of mutual funds Ramsey suggests inside the VA.

High-Income Earners

If a person earns too much to contribute to a Roth IRA and is limited to what he can contribute to a 401(k) plan due to top-heavy rules (unable to contribute 15% into pre-tax or tax-free investments), Ramsey recommends using either low-turnover mutual funds or a combination of low-turnover mutual funds and variable annuities. While this is an option for high-income earners, Ramsey still does not personally use variable annuities.

Worth Mentioning

Do not commit to VAs until ready. There is no getting out.

Never, ever, ever roll an IRA, 401(k), or 403(b) into a VA. These three things already have the benefit of tax-deferred growth, and a VA is not needed.

While Ramsey fits all the pre-requisites, for VAs he does not personally own any. He prefers mutual funds and paid-for real estate for investors on the last tip.

Investing for College

Ramsey recommends investing the first $2,000 per year in an Education Savings Account (ESA, Coverdell Savings Account). ESAs are very simple and work much the way a personal IRA does. When saving for a young child who will attend a public school, the ESA will usually be sufficient.

For investing more than this amount, or if income exceeds $200,000 annually, choose a 529 plan. The challenge with 529s is that every state has a different 529 plan and they all work differently. Some allow mutual funds; some require funds selection based on the child's age; while others are prepaid tuition programs.

When choosing a 529 plan, pick a program that allows funds selection up front and keeps those funds until time to use the funds for education. Remember to stick with the four types of funds Ramsey suggests. Do not use the pre-paid plans or ones that do age-based asset allocation.

Insurance

Long Term Care Insurance (LTC)

Ramsey recommends making LTC part of the plan at 60 years or older. LTC is a wise choice even provided there is a non-sizable estate to protect as long as the premiums are well within budget. For example, a 60-year-old couple with a full current income but a smaller estate may choose LTC simply for the quality of care it will provide them.

Disability Insurance

Ramsey recommends everyone purchase long term disability insurance to replace income in the event they are disabled. The cost of long-term disability depends on occupation. White-collar employees carry less risk than blue-collar employees and therefore are less expensive to insure. For short term disabilities (90 to 180 days), a fully funded emergency fund will cover your expenses, so Ramsey does not recommend purchasing short-term disability policies.

Life Insurance

Everyone should have 15-year (or longer) level term life insurance. Coverage should equal eight to 10 times annual income. The logic behind this is that a beneficiary could invest the entire amount into mutual funds and draw 8-10% annually as income without actually consuming the original insurance amount. Effectively, this replaces the revenue that was being generated by the deceased person. Never purchase any cash value or permanent insurance such as whole life, variable life, universal life. Never cancel any old policy until the replacement policy is entirely in force.

Exchange Traded Funds (ETFs)

Ramsey does not own ETFs and does not recommend them as part of any investment plan.

ETFs are baskets of single stocks that are intended to operate like mutual funds, but they are not mutual funds.

Separate Account Managers (SAMs)

SAMs are third-party investment professionals who buy and sell stocks or mutual funds on another' behalf. Ramsey prefers to stick with the team of managers in large, old, experienced mutual funds.

Real Estate Investment Trusts (REITs)

Ramsey does not own any REITs and does not suggest them as part of any investment plan. As a category, REITs do not perform as well as good growth stock mutual funds. Limit invest in REITs to no more than 10% of the total investment portfolio.

Equity Indexed Annuities

Ramsey does not own Equity Indexed Annuities and does not suggest them as part of any investment plan. Equity Indexed Annuities agree contractually to limit loss while limiting gains. Invest only the S&P 500 or a similar one, if necessary.

Thrift Savings Plan (TSP)

Ramsey suggests investing 60% in C; 20% in S; 20% TSP.

Values-Based Investing

Ramsey does not use a values-based investing approach. Here is why:

In values-based investing, pick between two similar mutual funds that align with one's beliefs—a good concept.

However, few of these funds stand up to Ramsey's criteria for picking mutual funds (a five-year or longer track record of strong rates of return, professionally managed by a team of mutual funds managers).

Commissions and Fees

Long-term, class A shares are much less expensive than B shares or C shares, so Ramsey recommends them.

Ramsey does not personally choose fee-based planning (paying 1% to 2.5% annual fees for a brokerage account). With an A share mutual fund, pay an upfront load of 5% to 6% once. However, with a fee-based account, also known as a wrap account, one agrees to pay a 1% to 2.5% fee every year—forever. With account growth, the 1% to 2.5% fee will add up.

Pay a Pro or Not

Ramsey still chooses to use a professional and suggests others do, too. Statistics show that "do-it-yourselfers" are quick to jump out of funds when they begin to underperform. An excellent professional advisor will remind choice selection and prevent buying high and selling low.

Why an Advisor

They advise. Clients make all decisions. .The client pays them for advice and the ability to teach enough to make smart decisions about investments. Clients do not hand over decision responsibility because they are a professional, or even if Dave Ramsey trusts them.

Retain ownership and responsibility for all final decisions. Do not invest in anything unless it can easily be explained to spouse how the investment works. Find an advisor that is easy to communicate. Take time to make a wise decision.

In this section of the chapter, we will provide some thoughts as to what age to start toward having a budget. Here is a product line by Dave Ramsey's:

KIDS & SCHOOL

Kids (3-12)

Teens

Graduates & Entering College

For Church Youth Group

For Schools

For Homeschool

CLASSES

Financial Peace University

The Legacy Journey

Spanish

Military

Foundations (High School)

Foundations (College)

Generation Change for Home (Teens)

Generation Change for Church (Teens)

There are some areas this information is available: family, church, school, and personal initiative. All are important. The most important is parents setting a Christian example. Kids remember what they see not what is said.

Dave Ramsey recommends investing for protirement after two things are completed: debt-free and saved an emergency fund of three to six months of expenses.

Three-fourths of the people on the Forbes list of the 400 wealthiest people in America say getting and staying debt-free is the most important thing to do when it comes to handling money. The full emergency fund ensures a cushion in case of an illness or job loss and that retirement funds stay where they are and keep growing.

Protirement Planning Tips by CNN Money

Save as much as possible as early as possible.

Set realistic goals.

A 401(k) is one of the easiest and best ways to save for retirement.

An IRA also can give savings a tax-advantaged boost.

Focus on asset allocation more than on individual picks.

Stocks are best for long-term growth.

Making tax-efficient withdrawals can stretch the life of one's assets.

Working part-time in retirement can help in more ways than one.

There are other creative ways to get more mileage out of retirement assets.

Protirement Experience

Start protirement planning at age forty.

Encourage children to start to save for a used car and a local college.

Fidelity Investments offered the most helpful tools for the process based on years of familiarity with Fidelity through a company 401(k). Fidelity provides many services. The following are personally beneficial:

Articles

Bill Pay

Full View (Balance Sheet & Net Worth)

Income Management Account (IMA)

Portfolio Advisory Service

Research

Retirement Planning

1040 Tax Transaction Transfer

Chapter Key Takeaways

Marriage, children, home, and cars are the most significant investments made in life. Take time, think, and pray about it.

A budget requires both spouses approval.

Always pay taxes and give charitable gifts first, then live on what is left.

Never spend more than one's income

Compound interest is either a mighty foe (Debt) or friend (Investment)!

The Church has a responsibility to provide life-stage lessons to assist with this vital life process.

Financial Health Estate

70% of Americans do not have a will.

Touching the Future: A Guide and Workbook for Estate Planning and Charitable Giving by the American Red Cross is an excellent additional resource.

Marriage or the birth of the first child is an excellent time to prepare a will and maintain it regularly. If single, as you begin to accumulate stuff is an excellent time to make a will and keep up to date annually.

Informational written by Dave Ramsey and Fidelity Investment is in this chapter.

Estate Planning, for some, is primarily tax driven. However, for the Christian steward, the estate planning process is relationship driven. We desire to be in a proper relationship in our stewardship trust given by God. Therefore we plan to assure that leaving assets behind blesses our family and our ministries—thus strengthening relationships rather than harming them.

For most, estate planning is not as complicated or costly as feared. For others, it can require complex documents and involve multiple professional authorities. In either case, good life stewardship includes a plan of distribution for when we no longer need the assets God has entrusted to us.

Essential to every estate plan is a will, health care directive and power of attorney. Dave Ramsey endorses USLegal. Since 1997, U.S. Legal Forms has offered cost-effective, state-specific legal forms on the Internet (www.uslegalforms.com/#).

Will

Necessary for every estate plan is a will:

It is a legal document drafted during one's lifetime.

It provides the opportunity to give a final testimony of Christian faith.

It revokes all previous wills made.

It authorizes payment of all debts and expenses related to final illness. It authorizes the payment of taxes by the estate.

It disposes of personal property according to one's desires, either through direct instructions in the will, or by reference to a letter of instructions.

It makes in-kind or fixed dollar distributions to family members or charitable organizations.

It distributes the remainder of the estate to individual and charitable beneficiaries.

It names a personal representative who is responsible for entering the will into probate and making distribution according to one's desires expressed in the will.

It can nominate the person preferred to serve as guardian of minor children and other persons in charge of custodial responsibility.

It empowers the personal representative to carry out the terms of the will, especially relating to the ability to sell, dispose of, moreover, liquidate property and to continue the operation of business interests.

It establishes trusts for the benefit of minor children or other individuals who have income responsibilities.

It names the trustee of any trusts established and empowers that person to carry out the terms of the trusts for their duration.

It can be used to waive bond.

Each state has strict laws regulating the execution and validity of the will. It is crucial to retain competent legal counsel, familiar with the laws of one's state of residence, to draft one's will.

Joint Ownership of Property

For smaller estates, joint ownership of property may be an excellent estate planning tool. It avoids probate and provides an orderly transfer of property between two individuals. However, care must be taken not to place too much wealth in joint ownership, eliminating the use of tax saving opportunities available with other estate planning tools.

Except for small estates, the use of a trust is usually more desirable.

Trust

The benefits of a trust:

Avoid estate taxes.

Provide management for property in case of disability.

Protect minor children from premature distribution of property.

Avoid ancillary administration of the estate, if a real property in more than one state.

Distinguish separate property from the community the property when one moves from one state to another, and for many other purposes, including income tax planning.

A trust can be confidential, can be used to avoid probate, and can provide coordination for an entire estate planning process. It is easy to establish and easy to change.

The trust estate plan combines with the will that transfers all remaining property to the trust at the time of death. The trust also transfers a durable power of attorney. A trust allows the individual holding power to place property into the trust, should one become incompetent.

Durable Power of Attorney for Property

The realities of life dictate that we must consider who will be in a position to manage a property in case of mental or physical disability before death. Relying on family members or friends to act under court-appointed conservatorship is usually unwise. It may affect interpersonal relationships, and unnecessary costs and restrictions.

The alternative is to grant the power to manage a property in case of disability to an individual or a bank trust department. Design a power of attorney to be in effect during incompetency. In other words, a trust can do just about anything that it is designed to do.

Durable Power of Attorney for Health Care

A separate power of attorney can be granted to an individual to make health care decisions during disability; an individual trusted to hold one's care and well-being as a priority.

A durable power of attorney for health care does not give authority to the named individual to declare one's inability to make decisions. However, it does grant specific authority to that individual to consent to or refuse treatment, physically and mentally unable to make that decision.

Directive to Physicians

A directive to physicians is the statement during a time of good physical and mental health that indicates whether one does or does not wish to be kept alive by heroic means if there is no hope for survival.

Life Insurance Contract

Liquidity: There are needs to pay final expenses, death taxes, or provide distribution to one family member involved in a business or farm. Life insurance may be the only way to guarantee that this money will be available, in the right amount, at the time needed.

Protection for Dependents: Life insurance is when there has not been sufficient time to accumulate assets. A life insurance policy designed to provide cash when needed most may be the only way a family can guarantee enough assets for the surviving spouse and children.

Charitable Estate Planning

Charitable gifts are to charitable beneficiaries as God's plan of stewardship for the estate to share part of the wealth that God has.

Once decided, the tax advantages of a charitable transfer and the integration of these transfers into the total estate plan can be of significant benefit to the overall strategy. Several tools are available.

Planned giving is a process that determines which giving technique will provide the most significant charitable potential to both the donor and the charity. It encompasses annual, special projects, and future gifts.

There are four types of donors:

Those who can make gifts now:

Cash
Real Estate
Personal Property (Appreciated Securities)

Those who can make gifts, if they receive income in return:

Charitable Gift Annuity

Charitable Remainder Unitrusts

Those who can make gifts, but only in the future:

Gifts From Will or Trust
Gifts of Life Insurance
Gifts From Retirement Plan
Gifts of Real Estate
Gifts of Personal Property

Those who want to preserve assets for their heirs:

Deferred Gift Annuity
Charitable Lead Trust

Business Estate Planning

There are additional estates planning tools available to the owner of a closely held business. Many advantages of these tools are related to the income tax structure of the company. Some that may be beneficial in estate planning may have income tax disadvantages. Their use may also be contingent upon the relationship of the business estate to the personal estate.

Incorporation

Many people own and operate small businesses, and family members are often involved. The incorporation of the company, combined with a program to make annual gifts of closely held corporation stock, may have excellent estate planning results. These include the tax-free transfer of future appreciation to family members while maintaining income and voting control.

In this is a complex area of planning tax and legal counsel should advise whether or not the incorporation of business is advisable. Incorporation may have drawbacks from income tax, workmen's compensation and unemployment insurance standpoints.

Partnership Agreements

Similar benefits are available by forming a partnership with family members. Family members are allowed to participate in the appreciation of the business. Like incorporation, this is a very complex area of planning. Again, rely upon legal and tax counsel advise.

Business Purchase Agreements

In business planning, it may be wise to consider aging with a business partner to buy one's shares of the business upon death. In exchange, the other partner would agree to purchase his or her stock of the company, should the partner predecease. The partner maintains control of the company, and the surviving beneficiaries of the deceased partner have a ready market for the business interest.

It is usually wise to fund a business purchase agreement with life insurance, to make sure that there is sufficient cash when needed most. The business purchase agreement can also be used to peg the value of the business interest in the estate, for federal estate tax purposes.

Special Use Valuation of Real Property

The law allows a particular use valuation method for real property devoted to farm or other closely held business use. This valuation method places a lower value, and thus a smaller estate tax on such property.

Some rules govern qualification for this valuation. Qualification depends upon the relationship of the property to the total estate value, management of the property before death, length of ownership, who receives the property, and restrictions on the sale of the property after death. However, when achieved these qualifications reduce estate taxes.

Redemption of Corporate Stock at Death

The Internal Revenue Code includes provisions for a corporation's redemption of stock from the estate. That stock is not taxable as a dividend, to the extent that distribution does not exceed the amount of the federal and state death taxes, interest on those taxes, and deductible funeral and administration expenses of the estate.

Again, restrictions must be noted. Hover, in many business estates, this is a valuable estate planning tool. These are but a few of the estate planning instruments available.

Taxation of the Estate

In 2017 Taxation of the Estates was eliminated.

State Death Taxes

There is a deduction against federal estate taxes for state death taxes paid. State inheritance tax: Many states have a tax on the right to inherit property. Those closely related to the decedent form one class, those less closely related form another class, and those separate form a third class. A different exemption is usually allowed for each class. Certain types of property may be exempt from state inheritance tax, such as life insurance, real estate held jointly with a surviving spouse. Local tax adviser, legal counsel, or bank trust department can furnish information relating to state inheritance tax implications locally.

State estate tax in place of an inheritance tax: Some states impose an estate tax that operates on a principle similar to the federal estate tax. The state imposes a permanent exemption or credit, and one tax rate (though it might be progressive) for all beneficiaries.

The Property Section

When making a listing of property, it is essential that clear instructions to planners as to the ownership of property. The basic types of property ownership are Individual ownership, Tenants in common, Joint tenants with rights of survivorship, Tenants by the entirety and Community property.

The success or failure of tax planning and the final distribution of one's estate are often dependent upon the coordination of property ownership with legal instruments in effect. It would not be practical to have appraisals made on all property at this time. However, it is essential to furnish professional counsel with reasonable values. Be realistic; do not over-value, or be too conservative. Give special attention to collections, hobbies, jewelry, and antiques. If there is any question on valuation or ownership, provide the professional counsel with as much information as possible.

Personal Representative Choices

The personal representative will be responsible for carrying out the terms of the will at the time of death. There are several items to take into consideration in the selection of this individual.

Availability: Many times, individuals wish to appoint a personal representative who lives some distance from the estate. An individual of approximately the same age or an individual occupied in business might not be available to handle the responsibilities of a personal representative. Be sure to consider a personal representative who will be available when needed.

QUALIFICATIONS: Is the individual being considered qualified for the job through experience, business management?

INTERPERSONAL CONFLICTS: Many times, the individual appointed is a family member or someone with a vested financial interest in the estate. The responsibilities as a personal representative may place him in a position of potential conflict with other family members.

The distribution of household goods and personal effects, the sale of the family home, a continuation of the family business or farm, all are decisions that may be better made by a third party, someone without a vested interest.

A good case can be made for the bank to serve as personal representative. A bank is bonded; they are available; they never move away or die. They do not have a vested financial interest in the estate, and they have experience in the probate process and management of estate assets. If personal involvement in decisions then a family member can serve with the bank, with powers limited to certain management decisions.

Remember, people are essential. Choose a representative carefully. When a bank or trust company are not, an alternate representative is needed.

Name/E-mail Address/Telephone

Personal
Representative_____

Alternate_____

Trustee

All that we have said concerning the choice of a personal representative can also be said about the choice of a trustee. The avoidance of interpersonal conflict, competence, and availability, all need to be taken into consideration.

Where a bank is selected and family representation, a co-trusteeship is possible. When given the power to change trustees or veto the action of the trustee, this is usually sufficient control to satisfy most estates.

Name/E-mail Address/Telephone

Trustee_____

Alternate_____

The realities of life dictate that we must give consideration to whom will be in a position to manage property and make health care decisions in case of mental or physical disability prior to death.

Relying on family members or friends to act under court-appointed conservatorship may affect interpersonal relationships and cause unnecessary costs and restrictions. The alternative is to grant this power to a trusted individual who holds one's care and well-being as a priority. This power does not give the named individual the ability to declare incompentcy. However, it does grant specific authority to that individual to act on one's behalf when one is declared incompetent

Name/E-mail Address/Telephone

Power for Property_____

Alternate_____

Health Care
Power_____

Alternate_____

Guardian for Minor Children

One of the most important reasons for a young family to have an estate plan is to name a guardian for minor children. It's impossible to replace parents, but if death occurs, someone must fill that place.

Select someone whose lifestyle is compatible, who will care for one's children in the kind of family surroundings that one desires, or the probate court will appoint the person. Selection of the person will be one the most difficult in the estate planning process.

The following guidelines may be of value to make this choice:

Individuals who do not have children may not make excellent guardians. Learn to be parents by being parents of babies, one-year-olds, five-year-olds. This experience is important.

Many people who have two children want two children. For this reason, they might not wish to be guardians, creating a larger family.

The age of the children of the family chooses as guardians are essential. They should be the same general age as one's children, avoiding a two-family situation.

Moreover, most importantly, make sure that the lifestyle of the people chosen is compatible with a Christian lifestyle, so the children will have the opportunity to continue to grow spiritually. When an individual is selected, discuss their willingness to serve.

The nomination of an alternate guardian is also essential, should the individual initially selected be unable or unwilling to serve when called.

Name/E-mail Address/Telephone

Guardian_____

Alternate_____

The Planners Section

Estate planning is not a do-it-yourself project. Competent counsel, with expertise in state law, tax planning, and estate draftsmanship, is extremely important.

If one has competent estate planning legal counsel, one is fortunate. Such legal counsel will be the key to one's estate planning team.

Other members of the team will be an accountant, life underwriter, investment adviser and bank trust officer. If one does not have competent legal counsel, another member of the estate planning team may be able to suggest an individual experienced in this specialized field.

Most communities also have a lawyer referral service, which can refer one to two or three attorneys who are competent in this field.

Name/E-mail Address/Telephone

Attorney_____

Financial Planner_____

Insurance Agent_____

Investment Adviser_____

Spiritual Leader_____

Family Physician _____

Human Resource Manager
(If employed)_____

The New Beginnings website (www.gonewbeginnings.net/) offers.

Funeral planning is an integral part of the estate planning process, performed as a labor of love to give guidance and direction to loved ones when they need it the most by relieving the emotional burden of decision-making and allowing them to support one's wishes regarding final plans. Most people should start thinking about pre-planning their funeral in their forties. Here is how to do it:

Write down funeral plans. Write down all the details, including the kind of service wanted (religious, secular), where and how you want to rest, whether or not you want a public viewing, and the funeral home you would like to use. Keep these directions in a safe place where the family can easily access them upon one's death. The Funeral Home and Commentary will have necessary forms.

Pre-pay for as much of the funeral cost as possible. Many funeral homes will allow pre-paying for the funeral service and related items, and many cemeteries will allow pre-paying for the plots. This way, the family will have little, if any, bills upon one's death.

Estate Document Locator

The organizer should include the following sections:

Financial accounts and records: car title, home ownership document, every active insurance policy, mutual funds, rental property, business ownership documents, college funds, financial statements, contact advisor directory.

Wills and estate plans

Information for all financial accounts

Recent tax returns and other documents: deeds, titles, birth certificates, passports, Social Security cards.

Funeral Instructions

Legacy letters to family members

Testimonial letter

Even in the most open families, the conversation often quiet when two subjects arise: death and money.

For both parents and adult children, confronting the prospect of each other's deaths can be uncomfortable. Privacy around financial matters is often a key concern, even among close family members.

Why conversation is critical:

When it comes to estate planning, there are often significant financial and personal benefits to being transparent and having sensitive conversations. For example, selected likely survivors would be comfortable managing a particular asset or serving as trustee when in reality that person is not up to the responsibility.

From the survivors' perspective, it is vital that they understand one's intentions and plans for the estate. Lack of clear communication during estate planning (or an inadequate or outdated plan) can not only reduce the amount your beneficiaries receive, but it can also result in uncertainty and conflict for them in an already stressful time.

If one does most of the work on family finances, be sure of the survivors' comfort level with taking on the task and their understanding of one's intentions. For some, it may be best for a professional to assume the responsibility. Consult with one's attorney or advisor.

Survivors may even make decisions based on erroneous ideas of what the deceased would have wanted. For example, when communication is lacking, some surviving spouses think honoring their loved one means keeping investments precisely as they were at the time of death. Eventually, this could lead to an outdated portfolio and missed growth opportunities.

Sometimes, to be effective, the conversation may need to extend beyond the immediate household:

As an adult child, make sure the parents have their plans and will be adequately cared for if one of them passes away or becomes incapacitated.

As a parent, make sure the children have an understanding of the plans and wishes; if the children are still minors, make sure the appointed guardians are willing and clear on one's intentions.

As a grandparent or other relative, ensure grandchildren, nieces, nephews will be taken care of through one's estate planning, as well as coordinating with their parents on their plans, too.

The benefits of having a dialogue about estate planning within the family do not stop at asset protection and an accurate understanding of intentions. Such an open discussion can:

Bring the family a sense of empowerment, by taking control of each other's collective future rather than leaving some elements to chance.

Passing-on of Family Values

Help the family develop a common understanding and a shared philosophy for a family's legacy for the generations.

Help prepare the family for family member incapacitation.

Help other members of the family— parents, siblings, or children— develop a responsible plan.

Allow the family to take advantage of some of the best tax strategies.

How to get the conversation started:

Despite how important this conversation can be, it may still be difficult to initiate. There is indeed more than one right way to begin a dialogue; however, here are a few suggestions for guidance:

Pick a specific, comfortable environment during a period of relative calm. Do not wait until a time of crisis when it may be too late to make adequate plans, and family members may not feel emotionally able to talk.

Be sincere about intentions. Be clear about initiating these talks out of concern that proper plans are in place and are understood.

Stress the importance and benefits of this conversation to everyone affected. One way to do this is to show an example of how an estate did not handle appropriately because family members had failed to discuss their plans with each other.

Chapter Key Takeaways

Prepare and review regularly:

Will

A revocable trust (if needed)

Power of attorney for Health Care

Power of attorney for Property

Memorandum of Tangible Property

Funeral Instructions

Animal Care Instructions

Legacy Letters

Testimonial Letter

Executive Instruction Letter

Estate Document Locator

Have a family discussion meeting

Have a sentimental property meeting

The Church has a responsibility to provide life-stage lessons to assist with this vital life process.

Financial Health Legacy

Who rather than Why

Legacy planning is more about who rather than why of current estate planning. It is value-based planning.

A legacy is the story of someone's life, the things they did, the places they went, the goals they accomplished, their failures, and more. Legacy is something that a person leaves for remembrance. Legacies are pathways that guide people in decisions with what to do or what not to do by wanting to leave a mark and create a legacy example for people to follow.

Leaving behind a legacy is essential for everybody. Heroes, villains, and everyday people leave behind a legacy that creates meaning in our lives. A grandmother's legacy may be relevant to her family. A family's heritage is a legacy that a person would be interested.

A legacy also leaves behind the story of a person so that they are not forgotten. Legacies are important pathways for the future to follow or to be guided by to make better decisions in life. Leaving behind a legacy gives us comfort in knowing that once we are gone, we will be in the memories of others.

The Legacy of Memories

Sharing or creating memories gives the family the gift of "you." Share stories about one' life, childhood, and teenage experiences. These stories let the family know more about one' past. They create a sense of history and heritage. Even if grandchildren do not fully appreciate stories now, it is likely they will come later in life, which thus creates that legacy of memories. Spending time with the family is also important – in a variety of life's settings – as these times will create memories that stick with the grandchildren, i.e., the "Power of Being There!"

The Legacy of Faith

The greatest legacy is the gift of faith. Model faith, letting them see what the Christian life looks like in real life. Talk about what faith in Jesus Christ means. Engage the family in a discussion about spiritual issues. Being a believer for a long time. Expressways faith has changed, been challenged and has deepened over the years. Throughout the years, as the family matures in principle, they will develop increased gratitude for the heritage of faith contributed!

The Legacy of Life

Make a note that the characteristics of real-life the fruits of the Spirit are in Scripture in Galatians 5:22-25. The attributes are love, joy, peace, patience, kindness, goodness, faithfulness, gentleness and self-control. In interactions with the family, model, speak about or praise these characteristics invests in driving these principles deep into their hearts, creating a desire for a Spirit-led and Spirit-fed life.

The Legacy of Love

Loving the grandchildren now will have a powerful influence on the kind of people they will grow up to become. Loving the grandkids

50

do not mean expensive gifts! Ultimately, the best demonstration of love is by presence and involvement in grandchildren's lives. Give them the gift of "yourself!" When physically not there be present through phone, notes, emails and the like. Love is powerful! Loving the grandchildren will make a lifelong difference! Never underestimate the power of a grandparent's love.

Legacy planning is anything handed down from one generation to the next. It can be heredity (green eyes), inheritance (dollars and cents), or heritage (spiritual). Spiritual legacy leavers are the most important, from the writer's perspective:

Make time for family

Know actions teach louder than words.

It is never too soon to begin teaching salvation and stewardship.

The local church is an ally.

Be happy and laugh a lot.

Vivian VanLier recommends the following protirement exercises and question:

Start a protirement planning journal. In, the journal place all ideas as they occur about "someday." Cut out pictures that represent the desired future and pastes them into the journal: images of places to travel, home and surroundings to look, of the work (whether paid or volunteer) you are doing. Are these pictures similar to life today, or different? Dream. Do not edit!

Set aside an hour or two. Meditate, listen to music, do what works to get relaxed. Now write in the journal about life 10, 20, 30 years from now. Include details describing a typical day, week, and month. Imagine living, friends, health, hobbies, working or not. Be creative, and concentrate. Do not edit!

Pretend to win the lottery and never have to worry about money again. Do not edit!

Make a list of things enjoyed doing. Look back and remember what it felt like to have a good time when too busy working and living life? Keep writing and add to the list remember joys from the past. Plan doing those things wanted but had no time. Add those to the list. Do not edit!

Remembering Your Story, by Richard L. Morgan, is an excellent resource to help one write a story. Kindle Direct Publishing is an inexpensive way to publish.

The author's elderhood protirement journey with God's help includes:

The Summit with Amy Hanson, Ph.D., gerontologist, and intergenerational ministry specialist, teacher, free-lance writer, speaker, consultant, author and mother of three

Founder of New Beginnings (gonewbeginnings.org/), a personal website dedicated to helping second-halfers' finish extremely well

Author of 14 books:

Second-Half Elderhood Protirement Ministry (Second Edition)

Longevity Response-Ability (Second Edition) Making an Aging Difference (Second Edition)

A New Life Stage (Second Edition)

Life Stages Lessons (Second Edition)

The Essential Ingredients for Second-Half Ministry; (Second Edition)

Planning the Life God Wants

Daily Legacy Living

Chism's Isms

The Second Half of Life

God's Grand Plan

Fundamental Retirement/Protirement Planning

Second-Half Ministry Seminary Curricula (Second Edition)

Answers for the Next Generation

Author on numerious guides:

Individual Aging Plan Guides

Early Life
Next Generation
Salvation
Marriage
Stewardship
    Budget
    Estate
    Legacy
Elderhood Protirement

Wellness
Finishing Extremely Well

Church Aging Guides

Church Health
Congregational Analysis
Aging and Development Ministry
Reading Certification Series

Aging Reading Certification, a reading program to assist church leaders in learning more about the issues related to the aging process and second-half ministry

Second-Half Ministry Position, a job description for elderhood, protirement, intergenerational, and development ministry.

The Longevity Response-Ability Crusade, a reform organizational action group for the second half of life equality and a better society

USA Missions Harvest Campaign, an initiative to equip 60 million second-halfers to evangelize 82 million unchurched

Second Half of Life Prayer and Commitment, a program to help create an age-integrated society

Sunday Flags Day, a witness to patriotism and religious freedom by flying the American and Christian flags each Sunday weather permitting

Prayer Corner to share issues and celebrate success stories.

Contributor to the forum on a new life stage, longevity response-ability, elderhood evangelism, and the second half of life equality

All royalties after expenses go to fund helping second-halfers.

Chapter Key Takeaways

Inter-family and inter-generation communication

Be happy and laugh a lot

Spend time together

Share life lessons and family stories

Coordinate sentimental property

Give back

The Church has a responsibility to provide the life-stage experiences to assist with this vital life process.

Mental Health Maintenance

An Attitude of Gratitude Equals Greater Health

"Rejoice always, pray continually, give thanks in all circumstances; for this is God's will for you in Christ Jesus," 1 Thessalonians 5:16-18 (NIV).

"The healthiest human emotion is not loved but gratitude. Gratitude increases immunities. It makes it more resistant to stress and less susceptible to illness. Grateful people are happy because they are satisfied with what they have. Cultivating an attitude of gratitude reduces stress in life and leads to greater spiritual and physical health, according Pastor Rick Warren.

This chapter has information from Jennifer Davis, *Healthy Aging Tips*, (2013).

Depression

While depression can be common in older adults, it is not a normal part of aging. A disorder that affects mood, feelings, behavior and even physical health, depression is a medical condition requiring attention.

Depression affects nearly 6 million Americans over the age of 65; however, only about 10 percent receive treatment, which means that the normal functioning of millions of seniors is interfered with daily. Among seniors, approximately 10 percent of primary care patients and nearly 20 percent of long-term care residents suffer from major depression, the most severe form of depressive illness. Suicide and depression are a cause and effect relationship linked with is almost six times higher for white males over the age of 85 than it is for the general population. Beyond its direct effects on senior's quality of life, depression is a risk factor for increased mortality and disability.

Depression is a biological illness that affects behavior, thoughts, and feelings. It is manifested as an intense feeling of sadness that may follow a loss or other traumatic event but is out of proportion to that event and persists beyond an appropriate length of time. Eran Metzger, M.D., says that most people get the "blues" now and then, but are not depressed. The following signs —can indicate depression:

Persistent sadness, anxiety or an "empty" feeling.

Feelings of hopelessness, helplessness, guilt or worthlessness

Have decreased energy and fatigue

Restlessness and irritability.

Difficulty concentrating, remembering or making decisions

Loss of interest in pleasurable activities

Persistent thoughts of suicide or death

Depression is treatable with antidepressant medications, psychotherapy, and self-help (e.g., meditation, relaxation techniques, and support groups). Also, developing a hobby, staying involved with activities that keep one's mind and body active, and maintaining in touch with family and friends are all proven ways of keeping major depression at bay. The good news, says Dr. Metzger, is that once depression is recognized and treatment sought, symptoms will lessen. About 60 to 80 percent of people diagnosed with depression are treated successfully outside the hospital.

Social isolation and loneliness, the presence of other illnesses such as Parkinson's, Alzheimer's, cancer or stroke, recent bereavement, the use of certain medications (some of which can cause or worsen the symptoms of depression), and family history of depression can increase a senior's risk of suffering from depression. Doctors and family members may miss the signs of depression in seniors. As a result, many seniors end up having to cope with symptoms that otherwise are treatable.

It is not unusual for older adults to experience sadness when faced with changes that are associated with aging; however, clinical depression may exist when persistent sadness does not lift, and this altered mood affects the individual's ability to function normally, says Eran Metzger, M.D.

Family members and doctors should look for the following signs if they suspect an older adult may be depressed:

Agitation

Anxiety

Social withdrawal

Decreased appetite

Unexplained weight loss or gain

Lack of attention to personal care

Sleep disturbance

Loss of interest in usually pleasurable activities

Feelings of discouragement or hopelessness.

A physical exam can determine if a medical illness is contributing to or causing the depression, while blood tests can rule out thyroid, kidney or liver problems, some of the symptoms of which can mimic depression. A psychiatric evaluation can help determine what depression is and what might be dementia, a significant loss of intellectual and cognitive function.

Medications such as selective serotonin reuptake inhibitors (SSRIs) and tricyclic antidepressants work by increasing the amount of the neurotransmitter serotonin, which plays a vital role in the regulation of mood, in the brain. Monoamine oxidase inhibitors (MAOIs) prevent the breakdown of serotonin but carry potentially dangerous side effects, so they are used infrequently.

Properly treating depression in older adults may help reduce the likelihood of death from physical illness, prevent suicide, and reduce health-care costs, which are nearly 50 percent higher for seniors with depression.

Most seniors are happy, content, and positive growing older. Others need assistance in helping them adjust to life's changes says Dr. Metzger. "Social interaction with family and friends can help them adjust to losses and change. Participating in activities, either alone or with others, can help keep seniors occupied and their minds engaged. Moreover, exercise is an effective measure to ward off depression or to prevent symptoms from worsening."

Memory Loss

Memory loss is not an inevitable part of aging. That said, many healthy individuals are less able to remember certain kinds of information as they age. Ruth Kandel, M.D., recommends the following tips for helping one's memory:

Be attentive; pay attention to remember.

Avoid fatigue; a good night's sleep will help strengthen memory.

Keep the brain healthy by treating medical problems, such as hypertension that may increase the risk of dementia.

Take preventive measures, such as wearing a seat belt, to protect one from injuries to the brain.

Keep a memory notebook with reminders.

Exercise; there is some evidence suggesting that regular, moderate exercise lowers the risk of dementia.

Use it or lose it; participate in cognitively stimulating exercises.

Treat sensory loss (i.e., vision and hearing) that can further isolate you.

Do not panic; anxiety exacerbates memory problems.

Ignoring memory loss says Dr. Kandel, may have substantial consequences beyond the frustration and embarrassment of not being able to remember things. If one is having memory problems, consult a physician.

Alzheimer's Disease (AD)

Alzheimer's disease is a chronic brain disease that accounts for approximately 60 - 80 percent of all dementias. AD is a progressive deterioration of memory, language, visual perception and activities of daily living. It can also be associated with depression, delusions, and hallucinations. One out of eight Americans age 65 and older are thought to have Alzheimer's, with the number climbing to nearly half of people age 85 and older. Risk factors include age and family history of Alzheimer's. Ruth Kandel, M.D., says that there are some reasons to screen for Alzheimer's disease, including early treatment, patient safety, and caregiver stress. Also, potentially reversible causes, as well as annoyances of cognitive impairment, may be identified. Consider being screened for Alzheimer's when one or more of the following occur:

Misplace items frequently.

Have difficulty finding words.

Get lost easily.

Have memory loss that affects one's ability to function.

Have difficulty performing daily tasks.

Repeatedly ask the same question.

Show poor or decreased judgment.

Suffer behavior or mood changes.

Become disoriented to time and place easily. It is essential to see a clinician with expertise in this area to have a proper diagnosis and treatment plan started, says Dr. Kandel.

Choosing Care Providers

There are several options available when it comes time to provide a person with AD with more care than can be provided at home. Planning for a move to a facility requires forethought and careful consideration. Family members and caregivers need to determine which options are available, what type of facility will best meet the needs of the person with AD, and which costs and resources might be necessary to facilitate the move. The types of care settings vary but commonly fall into three main categories (Alzheimer's Association, 2012):

Assisted living facilities (also called board and care, or adult living, or supported care) provide a bridge between living independently and living in a nursing home. These facilities offer a combination of meals, housing, supportive care, and health care. The federal government does not regulate assisted living facilities, and definitions of assisted living vary from state to state.

Nursing homes (also called skilled nursing facilities, long-term care facilities, or custodial care) provide long-term care to individuals who require more intensive, ongoing supervision and care. These facilities have staff and services that address issues such as health care planning, recreation, nutritional concerns, medical care, and spirituality. The state licenses nursing homes and regulated by the federal government.

Alzheimer special care units (SCUs) are for the needs of Alzheimer's and other dementia patients in mind. These units can vary in form and may exist within various types of residential care facilities. Alzheimer's SCUs cluster individuals with dementia into groups on a floor or unit within a larger facility.

Caregivers

As the U.S. population ages, more and more families are faced with caring for an elderly, chronically ill, or disabled loved one. 22.9 million American households include caregivers, most of whom are women. Caring for a sick or aging relative is hard work, often taking a physical, emotional and financial toll on caregivers. Robin Bromberg, LICSW, recommends the following tips for taking care of one's self while taking care of a loved one:

Join a support group to share ideas and learn new caregiving techniques.

Identify issues that create the most anxiety and discuss them with the family.

Consider hiring a private geriatric care manager to assist.

Use stress management techniques to help relax.

Ask the church or synagogue if they have services or volunteers who can help.

Watch for signs of depression and seek professional help, if needed.

Use adult day or respite care services for a loved one to take a break.

Robin Bromberg, LICSW, says the National Family Caregiver Support Group (800-AGE-INFO) can provide information on how to access free advice and support on caregiving.

Stress

Stress is a physical, chemical or emotional response that causes bodily or mental tension. Hans Selye, the Canadian doctor who coined the term "stress," said: "Without stress, there would be no life." While we all experience stress in our lives, overwhelming and poorly managed stress can hurt our physical and mental health.

Eran Metzger, M.D., offers the following tips for reducing stress life:

Identify areas of stress and develop a plan for dealing with them.

Manage time effectively, giving priority status to the essential activities.

Simplify life by eliminating unnecessary tasks.

Practice relaxation exercises, including deep breathing, progressive muscle relaxation, visualization, and meditation

Exercise regularly and eat a healthful diet.

Think positively rather than focusing on negative thoughts and feelings.

Learn to be a good communicator by a clear expression of feelings, wants and needs.

Learn to say no — without feeling guilty about it.

Get a good night's sleep.

Recognize that drugs and alcohol do not reduce stress; instead, they increase dependency.

Develop a sense of humor to laugh at the ironies of the world.

Not all stress is harmful, says Dr. Metzger. Some stress, such as running a race, elicits a different biological response that may be beneficial.

Sleep Problems

Nearly 70 percent of American adults report frequent sleep problems. Sleep is essential for good health, mental and emotional functioning, productivity and safety. Eran Metzger, M.D., says the following steps can help one sleep better:

Go to bed at the same time every night, preferably not too early.

The bed is for sleeping; read or watch television in bed only as part of a bedtime routine if it helps relaxation to sleep.

Take a 10-minute break during the day for relaxation exercises or meditation; if necessary, try to nap at the same time every day for the same length of time.

Exercise in the morning or early afternoon

Spend 20 minutes in a warm bath before going to bed.

Ensure that the bedroom environment is conducive to sleeping, with room temperature, darkness, and noise control adjusted for comfort.

Eat a light dinner at least three hours before bedtime; a banana or glass of warm milk as a snack might have a sleep-inducing effect.

Avoid all caffeinated foods and beverages, even in the morning.

Remember, it is normal for older people to take longer to fall asleep and wake up briefly one to three times during the night; medication will not help and may cause confusion or daytime sleepiness.

Also, Dr. Metzger says certain medications sometimes cause daytime sleepiness, insomnia, or restlessness. If present, speak with a physician or pharmacist.

Feminization of Later Life.

Feminization of Later Life is a term that has been used to describe how women dominate older age groups and how their proportions increase with age. Older Americans are women. This diverse group varies in income, education, level of health, functional abilities, living arrangements, and access to support. By living longer than men, they face unique economic, social, and health challenges:

Inadequate income

Lack of health care access

Financial problems of long-term care

Chronic illness of heart, cancer, and stroke

Centenarians are the fastest growing segment in the population. Eighty-five percent are women. Instrumental to the longevity of this group is their individualism, strong sense of self-worth, and the ability to cope with losses, and remain optimistic.

Economic security is a critical issue for older women, especially those who are unmarried and living alone.

Since most women will live out their lives as widows, their primary source of income is Social Security. More than half of all senior women would be living in poverty without Social Security.

Most women are likely to be unemployed, work part-time, or work in industries that do not offer health insurance benefits. Aging women are at high risk of developing chronic and disabling diseases. Women are the primary recipients of long-term care.

Not all caregivers are young. Many are older or elderly that give as well as receive care. Many caregivers are also caring for children, older relatives, or grandchildren. Caregiving is physically tricky and brings with it financial, personal, and familial concerns.

It increases the risk of illness and injury for a group with little or no health insurance. Social factors (housing and living arrangements, transportation issues, education, and support systems) can significantly affect the health of older women. Friends, acquaintances, family, and social organizations are essential as support systems for the older woman. Support systems act as buffers to the effects of significant life events.

As women age, they often lose some of their support systems to death, relocation and work role changes. A growing number of women are volunteering and engaging in other activities to avoid isolation, maintain relationships, and keep active.

Chapter Key Takeaways

Attitude is a self-fulfilling prophecy:

Graduating into new beginnings

Creating a positive identity

Balancing greater freedom

Finding a new purpose for living

Relationships are the basis of meaningful connections:

Gender

Generation

Friends

Family (spouse, adult kids, grandkids, aged parents/in-laws, siblings, church)

Interests/recreation

Needs

Concerns/problems

Ethnicity/culture

Creative pursuits are the basis for meaningful redirection:

Continued learning

Purposeful activities

Financial opportunities

Encore career

Ministry vision

A constant attitude of gratitude

Be Happy!

The Church has a responsibility to provide life-stage lessons to assist with this vital life process.

Physical Health Disease Prevention

An Ounce of Prevention = a Pound of Cure.

This chapter has information from Jennifer Davis, *Healthy Aging Tips,* (2013) and Chauncey Crandall, M.D. *Fix It!* (2012), and Gerontology Certification course materials, (2012).

According to A Profile of Older Americans by ARRP, some of the more common health problems include:

Hypertension (37%)

Hearing Impairments (32%)

Heart Disease (30%)

Sinusitis (17%)

Cataracts (17%)

Orthopedic Impairments (16%)

Diabetes (9%)

Visual Impairments (9%)

Tinnitus (ringing in the ears) (8%)

Varicose Veins (8%)

Regular physical changes include the following:

A decrease in physical strength, endurance, and flexibility

The decline in the efficiency of body organs

Loss of bone mass

Slower reflexes

Taking longer to return to equilibrium

All the senses are affected to some degree as people age. The changes are particularly significant because it is through one's senses contact with the world occurs. The most impactful changes are those in hearing and vision.

When losses in these senses are significant, they can affect a person in several ways:

Communication and interaction with others

Mobility and independence

Perception of and response to the environment

Ease in accomplishing tasks

Self-image

How the brain works changes. Education and experience remain intact and even improve with age. On the other hand, learning and recall take longer, and it becomes more difficult to process multiple sources at the same time. Dementia is not typical in later life, but rather a disease that affects the entire population as a patient or caregiver.

There are many social changes in elderhood:

Loss, grief, and bereavement

Emotional Needs Later in Life

Retirement

Retirement represents a loss of stature, position, money, and authority. To retire acknowledges that one has become an old person. Fears of retirement are many. They include loneliness, poverty, sickness/chronic disease, death, and diminished mental capacity.

Regular Medical Check-Ups

Having regular medical check-ups is an excellent way to help stay healthy as one age. A 30-year-old does not necessarily have the same health issues as someone 60 or older. Robert Schreiber, M.D, says the doctor should review the body systems, including blood pressure, hearing, and vision, at a check-up every two years. This check-up should include a review of health risk factors, as well as behaviors that put one at risk for illness or injury. Also, the following should be checked regularly, depending on one's age:

Women should have, at a minimum, a cervical screening every three years after their first period.

Menage 35 and women age 45 should be checked every five years for blood cholesterol unlesss elevated, or have other risk factors.

Women between the ages of 50 and 65 should have an annual mammogram; women between 40 and 50 should check with their physician concerning how often they need a mammogram.

Both men and women age 50 require to be checked for colon cancer with a fecal occult blood test and flexible sigmoidoscopy annually, or with a colonoscopy every five years.

People age 65 and older should have regular medical check-ups, says Dr. Schreiber, which allows assessment of general health, as well as to modify behaviors—such as smoking, diet, and exercise—that can affect health and well-being.

Influenza

Influenza —more commonly known as "the flu" —is a viral infection that causes a fever, runny nose, cough, headache and body aches. Every year, flu outbreaks occur in the late falls or early winter, affecting thousands of people and causing illnesses that can last up to five to seven days or longer. Bed rest, drinking plenty of fluids, and avoiding exertion are the primary treatments of the flu. Some people with severe symptoms find relief from acetaminophen, ibuprofen or naproxen. On occasion, clinicians may prescribe anti-viral medication.

Ruth Kandel, M.D., says that having an annual flu shot is the best way to avoid contracting the influenza virus. While the flu shot is a good idea for all adults, the following people should make sure they are vaccinated against the flu every year:

Those with suppressed immune systems or have severe anemia.

Individuals with chronic conditions such as heart, lung and kidney diseases, or diabetes.

Residents of nursing homes or chronic care facilities

People 50 years of age or older.
Individuals employed in nursing homes, hospitals or other health-care settings.

Household contacts or people who provide home care to individuals who are at high risk for complications from influenza infection

The optimal time to get a flu shot is in October or November, just before the November-April flu season; however, says Dr. Kandel, if one misses having a shot in the fall, it is still beneficial to receive it at any time throughout the flu season. Individuals who are allergic to eggs should not receive the flu shot.

Eye Problems

It is no secret that, as we age, we have an increased risk of eye problems that can affect our lifestyle and independence. To minimize the chance of vision loss have regular eye exams that check for glaucoma, cataracts, age-related macular degeneration, and diabetic retinopathy. The likelihood of a good outcome is greater if these conditions are detected early. As we grow older, we all lose some vision. The most common eye disorders among older adults are Glaucoma, cataracts, age-related macular degeneration, and diabetic retinopathy.

Lynn Wittman, O.D., optometrist, suggests the following tips for maintaining eye health in growing older:

At age 40, have a full eye exam that includes an assessment of vision in each eye, screening for glaucoma, and dilation of the eyes to check for retinal damage.

Depending on the findings of on's initial screening, have annual testing for glaucoma or other eye diseases.

Eat a diet rich in green, leafy vegetables and take a multivitamin that contains vitamins A (beta-carotene), C and E, and zinc to help prevent the development or progression of macular degeneration, the leading cause of uncorrectable vision loss among seniors.

Protect eyes from the sun's damaging ultraviolet rays by wearing UV rated sunglasses.

Annually check eyes if one has diabetes, high blood pressure, a family history of retinal problems, or have suffered eye trauma, as these all increase the risk for eye disease.

Before going to sleep at night, apply a hot-water compress to the eyes for five minutes to flush out bacterial waste and congealed eye secretions that can cause eye surface disease.

Before going to sleep at night, apply a hot-water compress to the eyes for five minutes to help unblock the glands in the eyelids; this is helpful for dry eyes, a common condition as we age.

Also, says Dr. Wittman, one should see an eye specialist anytime a visual disturbances, redness in one or both eyes, swelling or pain in the eyes, or worsening vision.

Hearing Loss

Hearing loss is one of the most prevalent chronic health conditions in the United States, affecting people of all ages. According to the Hearing Alliance of America, more than 28 million Americans have significant hearing loss. Advancing age is the number one reason for hearing loss. While no formal guidelines exist for hearing screenings, Leesa Burke, M.A., F.A.A.A., recommends an initial screening at age 50. If no problem is detected, have another testing in five years. If otherwise, have annual testing.

"Yes" to two or more of the following, may indicate that your ears are not working as well as they should and that you should have a hearing test:

Others say the TV is too loud.

Understanding all the words is a problem.

Difficulty following a conversation in a crowd or noisy environment

Think that people are mumbling.

Frequent asking for another to repeat

Asking another person what was said.

Feel that others are talking too quietly.

Although most hearing loss does not cause right physical symptoms, says Ms. Burke, it does impact social relationships, emotional health, and overall well-being. Discovering and treating hearing loss can significantly decrease those effects.

Balanced Weight

Being overweight or underweight can cause serious health risks. By maintaining healthy body weight, the risk for certain diseases, including diabetes, stroke, high blood pressure, high cholesterol, and heart disease, may decrease. Healthy body weight is key to a healthy life.

There are several ways to determine a healthy weight for one's body. The easiest and least technical is looking in the mirror and assessing body fat (especially the location) and muscle tone. A more scientific measurement is Body Mass Index, or BMI, which compares weight to height to normal. A doctor can also help determine healthy body weight.

Susan Kalish, M.D., recommends the following ways to maintain a healthy body weight:

Eat an assortment of foods, including fruits, vegetables, grains, fish and poultry.

Evaluate what and how one eats.

Exercise regularly.

Eat sensible portions.

Gradually lose or gain weight. Be dedicated about losing, gaining or maintaining weight based on one's situation.

Also, says Dr. Kalish, seek the advice of a registered dietitian or physician when needed trustworthy, accurate, timely and practical information on maintaining healthy body weight or other nutrition issues.

Teeth Care

The nation's oral health, the best it has ever been, is essential to general health and well-being.

There are safe and effective measures to prevent the two most common oral diseases: dental caries (cavities) and periodontal disease (gum disease). Dr. Joseph Calabrese says the following are good ways for maintaining oral health:

Visit the dentist every three to six months to keep the overall health of teeth and mouth and provide for early detection of precancerous or cancerous lesions.

Practice good oral hygiene, including careful brushing at least twice a day and daily flossing.

Drink fluoridated water and use fluoride toothpaste to protect against dental decay.

Avoid tobacco products, which increase the risk of periodontal disease, oral and throat cancers, and oral fungal infections. Limit alcohol consumption (excessive consumption is a risk factor for oral and throat cancers).

Sudden changes in the sense of taste or smell or any changes to teeth or gums seek professional care.

Regular dental exams are crucial to the prevention of tooth decay, gum disease, and other dental disorders, as well as for the detection of oral cancers, says Dr. Calabrese.

Many times, a dentist or hygienist can detect a problem before a patient is even aware of it.

Blood Pressure

High blood pressure affects approximately 73 million Americans, nearly one-third of whom are unaware they have high blood pressure. It is a significant risk factor for heart disease, kidney disease, and stroke, contributing to more than 275,000 deaths each year. Blood pressure is a measurement of the forward thrust of blood against artery walls produced when the heart pumps blood to the rest of the body. The Joint National Committee on Prevention, Detection, Evaluation, and Treatment of High Blood Pressure, supported by the National Institutes of Health, divide blood pressure into these categories:

Class Systolic Blood Pressure

Diastolic Blood Pressure

Normal Less than 120 mm Hg AND

Less than 80 mm Hg

Pre-hypertension 120-139 mm Hg OR

80-89 mm Hg

Hypertension Stage 1 140-159 mm Hg OR

90-99 mm Hg

Stage 2 Greater than 160 mm Hg OR

Greater than 100 mm Hg

Robert Schreiber, M.D, says check blood pressure annually and possibly more often if one has borderline high or high blood pressure.

He recommends the following for keeping blood pressure under control:

Take blood pressure medications as prescribed.

Quit smoking.

Reduce sodium intake.

Exercise regularly.

Maintain an appropriate body weight.

Keeping blood pressure under control says Dr. Schreiber, is vital for maintaining overall health.

Cholesterol

It is common for cholesterol production to become excessive as we age. High cholesterol levels are widespread because we absorb it from certain foods we eat. Once absorbed into the bloodstream, cholesterol is broken down into LDL (bad cholesterol) and HDL (good cholesterol). While LDL can cause plaque buildup on artery walls, HDL helps reduce plaque.

A total cholesterol count of less than 200 mg/dL is optimal; however, the levels of LDL and HDL are more important indicators of cardiovascular disease risk. An optimal LDL level is less than 100 mg/dL, especially for those with heart disease, diabetes or vascular disease. High LDL and low HDL increase risk for heart disease. Unfortunately, HDL levels typically fall with age, particularly among women. Dr. Jennifer Rhodes-Kropf offers the following tips to keep cholesterol in check:

Take cholesterol medications as directed by a physician.

Maintain a healthy body weight.

Cut saturated fats (red meat, butter) and replace them with fish, poultry and low-fat dairy products.

Eat foods high in monounsaturated fats, such as olive, canola and peanut oil.

Exercise regularly.

Dr. Rhodes-Kropf says to have cholesterol checked every five years beginning at age 20 and more frequently if one has high cholesterol or other cardiovascular disease risk factors, especially diabetes.

Skin Care

Despite the natural process of skin aging — becoming less elastic, drier and more wrinkled —there are measures one can take to help minimize this process.

While age is one factor, family history, genetics, and behavioral choices all play a role in how our skin ages. Of particular importance is sun exposure, which causes most skin changes as we age. Dr. Jennifer Rhodes-Kropf offers the following tips to keep skin healthy:

Avoid intense exposure to sunlight by staying out of the sun when it is at its strongest (10 a.m. to 4 p.m.).

Use sunscreen with an SPF (sun protection factor) of at least 15 — higher is even better — applying it liberally and often, and after swimming (even with waterproof sunblock).

Wear protective clothing, such as loose-fitting items with tightly woven fabric, a wide-brimmed hat, and sunglasses.

Quit smoking; smoking increases wrinkles and the risk for squamous cell skin cancer. Topical creams, lotions, and gels can also help skin to age more healthfully, says Dr. Rhodes-Kropf. Speak with a dermatologist before using these products.

Osteoporosis

Osteoporosis and low bone mass, conditions that increase the risk of bone fractures, are major public health threats for an estimated 44 million American women and men 50 years of age and older. Women, especially those with small body frames and a family history of the disease, are most at risk of developing osteoporosis. Other risk factors include a diet low in calcium and Vitamin D, cigarette smoking, heavy caffeine use, menopause, drugs such as prednisone (used to treat arthritis), and a sedentary lifestyle. Douglas Kiel, M.D, says a bone densitometry test is one of the best ways to assess susceptibility to osteoporosis and bone fractures. The lower the score, the worse bone density. Women should have a bone densitometry test if they:

Are over the age of 65.

Are postmenopausal, with at least one risk factor besides osteoporosis or a bone fracture.

Have a family history of bone fractures or osteoporosis.

Are being treated with osteoporosis medications.

Are considering osteoporosis therapy.

Are menopausal and under the age of 65 and the test will have an impact on decision making regarding prevention.

Also, says Dr. Kiel, identification of women and men with low bone density and those at risk of falls are the best fracture prevention strategies.

Each year, nearly 320,000 Americans, most of them women over the age of 65, are hospitalized with hip fractures. Only 25 percent of these patients recover completely. Many patients require extensive rehabilitation or home care after a hip fracture. Douglas Kiel, M.D, says there are some steps people can take to reduce their risk of fracturing a hip:

Have a bone density test to assess the risk of fracture better.

Get enough calcium; depending on one's age and gender, between 1,000 mg and 1,500 mg per day.

Include at least 2,000 international units (IU) of Vitamin D in your diet per day.

Exercise regularly, including weight training, to minimize bone loss and strengthen muscles.

Eliminate smoking and excessive alcohol consumption.

Consult a physician about the need for osteoporosis medications.

Speak with a doctor about balance problems, which may cause falls.

Talk to a doctor about discontinuing or changing medications that make one dizzy or drowsy.

Eliminate hazards in the home, including loose rugs, electrical wires, and poor lighting.

Use an assistive device, such as a cane or walker, to help with mobility only if a physical therapist or physician correctly prescribed it.

Pneumonia

In the United States, about 2 million people develop pneumonia each year. Pneumonia is often the final illness in people who have other acute, chronic diseases. While several antibiotics, including penicillin, are effective at treating bacterial pneumonia, a vaccine is available that protects up to 70 percent of those vaccinated from severe pneumococcal infections. Ruth Kandel, M.D., says the pneumonia vaccine — which only protects against pneumonia caused by the pneumococci bacteria — usually lasts a lifetime. However, some people at highest risk may need another vaccination after five years. She recommends the following people be vaccinated:

Anyone over the age of 65

People with a chronic illness, such as diabetes and heart or chronic lung disease

Individuals with weakened immune systems (e.g., individuals with leukemia)

People who have had their spleen removed or whose spleen does not function properly (the spleen helps fight this type of pneumonia).

Those who have had an organ or bone marrow transplant

Individuals with chronic renal failure.

Alcoholics.

Dr. Kandel says that people who have had a severe reaction to this vaccine or one of its components should not have it again.

Osteoarthritis

Osteoarthritis is the most common form of arthritis, affecting more than 20 million Americans, most of the older adults. Osteoarthritis is a joint disease that affects cartilage, the slippery tissue that covers the ends of bones in a joint. As the surface layer of cartilage wears away, bones rub together and cause pain, swelling and loss of joint motion. The knees, hips, finger joints, the base of the thumb, neck and lower back are the most commonly involved. Dr. Marian Hannan gives the following tips for managing osteoarthritis:

Exercise — regular, moderate activity can help to increase joint range of motion, strength, and flexibility.

Rest — know when to slow down or stop; relaxation techniques, stress reduction, and biofeedback may be helpful.

Control weight — excess weight can overstress weight-bearing joints and exacerbate symptoms; even losing 8 to 10 pounds makes a big difference in arthritis symptoms.

Try non-traditional remedies — acupuncture is a useful component in some patients' treatment.

Consult with a doctor about medications to manage pain.

Also, says Dr. Hannan, focus on abilities rather than disabilities. Developing a support system with family, friends, health professionals, and support groups will help. While they are vital to maintaining health, both prescription and non-prescription medications can be dangerous if not used properly.

Medication Safety

Dr. Joseph Li recommends the following tips for practicing medication safety:

Take medications exactly as prescribed by a physician, and follow all instructions on the label.

Do not change the dosage or frequency without consulting a health-care provider.

Learn about the medications one is taking, including side effects and adverse reactions.

Do not share prescription medications with anyone else.

Do not take more than the recommended dose of over-the-counter drugs.

Report other medications taken to the pharmacist and physician to check for interactions. If one experiences side effects, contact a physician immediately.

Store medicine in the proper environment.

If a dose is missed, consult a physician or pharmacist on how to proceed.

Check expiration dates on all medication containers and discard those that have passed the listed time.

Keep all medications out of the reach of children.

Also, keep a physician's and pharmacist's phone numbers handy to contact with questions or concerns. Keeping accurate medical records, if one has a chronic illness, is an essential part of one's health care. Most states require physicians or hospitals to release a copy of one's medical records upon written request for a small fee. Regulations about the release of psychiatric or psychological records may vary from state to state.

Medical Records

Robert Schreiber, M.D., recommends keeping the following medical records at home for easy access:

An underlying medical history, including major medical problems such as chronic or acute illnesses, prescription medications, allergies, surgeries, hospitalizations (with dates), major accidents or injuries, and a list of blood relatives with significant medical problems.

Current prescription medications, including names of drugs, dosages, the reason for taking the medication, and the prescribing physician's name

A list of over-the-counter medications currently being taken

A list of prescription medications taken in the past.

A surgical history, including dates and locations of surgeries and surgeons' names

A list of physicians' names, addresses, and telephone numbers

A copy of one's living will, advance directives, or health-care proxy.

Remember, says Dr. Schreiber, to update records as changes occur. Research has shown that maintaining social engagement may contribute to longer and healthier lives. A Swedish study found that having a secure social network may lower the risk of developing age-related memory loss. Moreover, a study conducted by Hebrew SeniorLife's Institute for Aging Research showed that survival rates among socially active long-term care residents were higher than they were for those who were not.

Socially Active Life Style

Older adults can find ways to enjoy social connections, no matter what their physical limitations. The following describes a variety of ways elderhood adults can maintain a socially active lifestyle:

Get out of the house regularly.

Utilize older adult transportation available in the community to attend social gatherings and pursue interests.

Join civic, social or other organizations.

Go to church or temple.

Get together with family or friends.

Attend a structured daily adult day health program that offers programs and activities.

Enroll in a mall-walking club.

Participate in programs run by the community's senior center or council on aging.

Sign up for a "friendly visitor" to visit you at home.

Join an intergenerational program in the community.

Volunteer with a local non-profit organization, such as a school, library or hospital

In addition to its health benefits, Ms. Kaytis says remaining socially active also contributes to older adults' quality of life.

Hypothermia & Heat Stress

Brought on by extreme temperature, hypothermia (low body temperature) and heat stress (high body temperature) can cause life-threatening emergencies if not treated immediately. Older adults, especially those who are sick, frail and very old, are more vulnerable to extreme temperatures than younger people. Robert Schreiber, M.D., offers the following tips for dealing with temperature extremes:

COLD

Insulate one's home correctly; caulk windows to prevent drafts.

Wear layers of warm clothing, including a hat and scarf, to prevent heat loss through the head.

Use extra blankets at bedtime, as hypothermia can develop during sleep.

Eat nutritious foods, exercise moderately, and get an adequate amount of sleep.

Drink plenty of fluids.

HEAT

Keep as fresh as possible.

Stay in an air-conditioned environment, either at home or in a public place such as a shopping mall, movie theater, or library.

Use fans to draw fresh air into the house at night and circulate indoor air during the day.

Wear loose-fitting, lightweight clothing.

Curtail extreme physical activity.

Drink plenty of fluids.

Living alone, Dr. Schreiber says, have a relative or neighbor check in with you daily to make sure all is okay.

Emergencies

Emergencies can — and often do — strike without warning, whether a natural disaster such as a tornado, hurricane, earthquake or flood, an injury or medical emergency, or a fire. Preparing the house for an emergency, even if one never occurs, is essential for safety and well-being.

Lorraine Manjikian, an occupational therapist, recommends the following ways to make sure the house is emergency prepared:

Place emergency phone numbers— fire, police, ambulance, poison control, local hospital, personal physician for all household members, whom to call in an emergency—in a prominent place in the house, near a telephone; make sure that each household member knows where it is.

Keep a well-stocked first aid kit, with bandages, tape, alcohol, hydrogen peroxide, antiseptic, some form of pain reliever, scissors, tweezers, and a knife.

Develop a fire safety plan.

Install and maintain smoke detectors, carbon monoxide detectors, and fire extinguishers.

Store a three-day supply of water in plastic containers (one gallon per person per day).

Stock a three-day supply of non-perishable food items, including food for infants, seniors and people with special diets.

Keep an extra supply of prescription medications, such as insulin or high blood pressure medication.

Remember to stay calm when calling 911 during an emergency, says Ms. Manjikian, and give essential information, including the location and type of emergency and name, address, and telephone number.

Fall Safety

One out of every three Americans over the age of 65 falls each year. Among older adults, falls are the most common cause of injury and admission to the hospital for trauma and the leading cause of death from injury in the over-65 population. Also, falls account for 87 percent of all bone fractures in this age group.

Lewis Lipsitz, M.D., offers the following tips for helping to prevent falls:

Eliminate tripping hazards by removing scatter rugs, taping down electrical and telephone cords, and replacing plush carpeting with a thinner pile carpet.

Install handrails on both sides of staircases, as well as light switches at both the top and bottom of the stairs.

Have grab bars installed in the bathroom near the toilet and the tub or shower stall.

Sit in straight-backed chairs with hard seats, which are easier to get out of that soft, cushiony seating.

Have vision and hearing checked annually.

Take medications as ordered by the physician, and be careful of interactions with other drugs.

If you feel weak or dizzy after meals or when standing up, ask the doctor to check blood pressure after these activities to detect large drops in blood pressure that can cause falling or fainting.

While falls are a serious health problem among seniors, Dr. Lipsitz says taking the necessary precautions can go a long way in reducing the likelihood of falls occurring both within and outside of the home.

Personal Car Driving

The motor vehicle is the primary means of transportation in the United States. For all its advantages, the number of deaths and injuries resulting from motor vehicle crashes is staggering: more than 37,000 deaths and 2.5 million injuries in 2008. As we age, several common factors—visual acuity, diminished hearing, changes in physical strength, possible cognitive problems, and slower reaction times— affect our ability to drive.

Eran Metzger, M.D., who frequently deals with older-driver issues, recommends the following tips for safe driving as one age:

Have vision and hearing checked regularly.

Wear a seat belt at all times, as a driver and as a passenger.

The plan is a driving route and allows additional time to arrive safely.

Travel on familiar roads, avoiding rush-hour traffic and inclement weather.

Avoid driving at night if one has vision difficulties.

Understand the effects medication may have on driving.

Increase following distance to improve your reaction time.

Reduce distractions such as the car radio or cell phone.

Enroll in a driver-safety program offered by organizations such as the AARP, AAA and the National Safety Council. Dr. Metzger says that deciding to give up driving is an "important landmark" in losing your independence.

With proper planning, alternative methods of transportation can prevent seniors from having to forfeit most of their usual activities. Speak with family and friends and make an informed choice about continuing to drive.

Cancer

With early and regular screening, most cases of cervical cancer are correctable. In fact, with the advent of the Pap test, a screening test for malignant and premalignant changes to the cervix, the incidence of cervical cancer in the United States has been reduced by 75 percent over the past 50 years. Jennifer Rhodes-Kropf, M.D., says three ways to screen for cervical cancer exist: Pap tests, with follow-up tests if the results are abnormal but inconclusive; colposcopy, in which the cervix is examined and sometimes biopsied; and a test for human papillomavirus (HPV), the chief cause of cervical cancer. Based on recently-published guidelines, women should keep in mind the following regarding cervical cancer screening:

> Have regular Pap tests, even if post-menopausal; check with one's doctor concerning how often a test is needed.

> If a test is abnormal, one's doctor should follow-up with a colposcopy and HPV test.

Women should have tested for cervical cancer beginning at age 18 or the onset of sexual activity, says Dr. Rhodes-Kropf. Women should also speak with their doctor if they have questions or concerns about cervical cancer and screening methods.

Mammography, an X-ray to detect or diagnose changes in a woman's breast, is a front-line measure in breast cancer screening. Mammography plays a central role in the detection of breast cancer because it can show changes in the breast, such as lumps, up to two years before a woman or her doctor can feel them. Risk factors for breast cancer include a personal or family history of the disease, genetic alterations of the BRCA1 or BRCA2 genes, early onset of menstruation (before age 11), late menopause (after age

55), and no history of childbearing. Also, as women age, their risk for breast cancer increases. Jennifer Rhodes-Kropf, M.D., recommends the following National Cancer Institute guidelines for mammography:

Beginning at age 40, a woman should have a mammogram every two years.

Women at higher-than-average risk for breast cancer should talk to their doctor about screening before the age of 40, as well as the frequency of testing.

Have annual clinical breast exams.

Breast self-exams should be done monthly to detect any changes.

Studies have shown that breast cancer screening with mammography reduces the number of deaths from breast cancer for women ages 40 – 69, especially those over 50. No studies have been conducted yet for women under 40, says Dr. Rhodes-Kropf.

Younger women should speak with their doctor if they have questions about breast cancer screening. Nearly 187,000 new cases of prostate cancer are detected in the United States each year, and more than 28,000 American men die annually from the disease. It is the leading cause of cancer deaths in men over the age of 55. If prostate cancer is caught early through a PSA (prostate-specific antigen) test and digital rectal exam (DRE), new treatments make it possible for men to live longer and healthier lives following diagnosis. Howard Nachamie, M.D., offers the following recommendations for PSA tests and digital rectal exams:

> If one is at high risk for prostate cancer (if you are African- American or have a first-degree relative with prostate cancer), have an annual PSA test and DRE beginning at age 40.

> If one is over 50 and not considered to be at high risk, discuss testing with one's physician to determine if it is appropriate.

> Beginning at age 40, have an annual digital rectal exam.

> A PSA of less than four ng/mL is considered normal; however, changes over time can indicate a problem, even if the PSA is "normal." The PSA test is not perfect; individuals with cancer can have a normal PSA, and men without cancer can have a high PSA (usually due to enlarged prostate). A doctor can help one understand what PSA level means.

Also, women should have an annual digital rectal exam beginning at age 40, says Dr. Nachamie. DREs can detect rectal masses and blood in the stool, as well as help evaluate abdominal, genital and urinary complaints in both men and women.

Geriatricians

Geriatricians are medical doctors trained to deal with the unique needs and conditions of older adults. They are primary care physicians who have completed a residency in internal or family medicine, followed by a one or two-year fellowship offering specialized, in-depth training in the treatment of older adults. Robert Schreiber, M.D., says one may want to choose a geriatrician as one's primary caregiver as one age, especially if one has significant impairments. Here are some tips to follow in selecting a geriatrician:

Develop a list of characteristics wanted in a primary caregiver.

Ask friends who see a geriatrician for recommendations.

Check with the local Council on Aging or the American Geriatrics Society for a list of geriatricians in the area.

Choose a doctor who is board certified in either geriatrics or internal medicine.

Contact the offices of likely candidates and ask to schedule a brief interview with the doctor.

During the interview, assess comfort level and ability to communicate with the geriatrician and whether or not he or she understands one's health-care goals and concerns.

Determine if one's medical plan covers the geriatrician. Not all seniors need a geriatrician as their primary caregiver, says Dr. Schreiber. If one does not have significant impairments or special medical considerations, one may want to continue seeing one's current physician, especially if one has an established relationship and the physician knows one's medical history. Please be aware that geriatricians practicing primary care are few, and it can be challenging to get in to see one. Good communication between the doctor is critical to high-quality health care. Building a successful relationship with the doctor, however, takes time and effort. Robert Schreiber, M.D., suggests the following ways to get the most out of visits with one's doctor:

Be prepared— bring a list of questions one wants to ask; make a list of symptoms; bring one's medical records or have them transferred if seeing a new doctor.

Speak up — ask questions and get satisfaction answered; do not be embarrassed to discuss sensitive topics.

Disclose all information — tell one's doctor all one's symptoms, all the medications (prescription and over-the-counter) you are currently taking, and if any other healthcare provider is treating you.

Bring someone—a friend or family member can provide moral support and help relax, as well as help recall what the doctor said in the next appointment; this is especially important for seniors.

Follow-up — if one has questions or concerns after the appointment, call the doctor's office for clarification; if one wants to speak directly with the doctor, be patient but assertive. Bring advance directives—this document outlines one's wishes for medical treatment in the event of incapacitation.

Also, Dr. Schreiber says to ask the doctor about what health screenings are appropriate for one's age. Many people confuse hospice and palliative care, thinking they are the same. Although they share a similar philosophy, the delivery of care is different. Both hospice and palliative care focus on the quality of life or "comfort care," including the active management of pain and other symptoms, as well as the psychological, social and spiritual issues often experienced at the end of life.

Hospice and Palliative

David Tsai, M.D., explains the following similarities and differences in hospice and palliative care:

HOSPICE CARE

A Medicare benefit, hospice is available for patients whose life expectancy is six months or less, as determined by their physician.

Patients must sign a form acknowledging that they will forgo curative efforts.

Hospice care takes place in the home, long-term care facility, or hospice residence.

Hospice extends to the family into the period of bereavement.

Palliative care

Palliative care services do not depend on life expectancy and are in conjunction with curative efforts.

Palliative care is generally hospital-based and in long-term care facilities.

Services generally do not provide bereavement care. Families should speak with their physician early on about prognosis and goals of care, and ask about contacting a hospice or palliative care service.

Major Disease Killers

Approximately two million American's die from heart disease, cancer, lung disease, stroke, accidents, Alzheimer's Disease, diabetes, kidney disease, influenza and pneumonia, and self- harm in 2010. Heart disease and strokes are the nation's leading killers, accounting for 33% of all deaths.

In the early 1970s, researchers began investigating the cardiovascular benefits of daily aspirin therapy. They found that daily aspirin substantially reduces the risk of death and non-fatal heart attacks in individuals who have had a previous heart attack or unstable angina, which often occurs before a heart attack.

Today, the American Heart Association recommends low-dose daily aspirin for people who have had a heart attack, have unstable angina or are at high risk of having a heart attack. However, James R. Jewell, M.D., cautions that daily aspirin therapy is not for everyone and suggests the following guidelines:

Take daily low-dose aspirin only after consulting one's doctor.

Take only baby aspirin (one or two, depending on your doctor's recommendation); regular-strength aspirin is more likely to cause gastrointestinal bleeding.

Do not take aspirin if taking other anticoagulants, or allergic to aspirin without consulting one's doctor.

Do not replace aspirin with acetaminophen or ibuprofen. Do not combine the above without directions.

Chest pain might be a heart attack, chew an aspirin (regular strength) as soon as possible; studies have shown that this improves outcome.

Dr. Jewell says risk factors for a heart attack by not smoking, exercising regularly, watching cholesterol and blood pressure, maintaining proper body weight, and reducing stress.

A heart attack happens when the flow of oxygen-rich blood to a section of heart muscle suddenly becomes blocked, and the heart cannot get oxygen. Restore blood pressure quickly to help heart muscle beginning to die.

The Top Risk Factors for Heart Disease

Age 65 or older

Depression

Diabetes

Excessive drinking

A family history of heart disease

High blood pressure

High cholesterol

High stress

Obesity

Poor nutrition or dietary habits

Sedentary lifestyle

Smoking

Pre-Heart Attack Symptoms

Unusual fatigue

Sleep disturbance

Anxiety

Pain in the shoulder blade or upper back

Sweating

Irritability

Top Heart Attack Warning Signs

Chest Pain

Shortness of breath

Indigestion or Heartburn

Nausea and Vomiting

Additional Heart Attack Signs

The discomfort that spreads to the shoulders, arms, back, neck or jaw

A choking feeling

Profuse sweating

Rapid or irregular heartbeat

Dizziness, weakness, or lightheadedness

A vague, general sense of illness

Anxiety or a sense of doom

Passing out

Preventive Steps for a Heart Attack

Eat a healthy diet

Engage in physical activity every day

Limit alcohol

Lower blood pressure to less than 120/80 mmHg

Maintain a healthy weight

Manage diabetes (people with diabetes are two to four times more likely than non-diabetics to develop cardiovascular disease)

Reduce blood cholesterol to less than 200 mg/dL

Reduce stress

Stop smoking

Heart Lifestyle Tips

Exercise (Age 18 to 65)

Thirty minutes of moderate-intensity aerobic physical activity, such as brisk walking, five days a week.

Twenty minutes of vigorous aerobic activity, such as jogging, three days a week Light exercise as part of a daily routine Take the stairs, do yard work or walk around while on the phone.

Diet

Add more to one's diet (25 to 30 grams per day) by eating raw vegetables and fruits, whole grains and beans.

Consume lean meats and poultry and remove the skin.

Consume less than 6 grams of salt per day.

Cut back on foods containing partially hydrogenated vegetable oils or "trans fats," such as hard margarine and shortening, and most baked goods.

Eat at least two servings of fish per week.

Limit alcohol consumption to one drink per day for women and two drinks for men.

Switch from whole-fat to low-fat or non-fat dairy products.

Monitor Your Heart Health

Blood pressure

Blood sugar levels

Body mass index (BMI)

Cholesterol levels (Total, HDL, LDL, and triglycerides)

Waist circumference — a man with a waste of more than 40 inches or a woman with a waist of more than 35 inches, are considered high-risk

NOTE — Except BMI and waist measurement, these tests should be performed by a doctor or under a doctor's supervision. Online risk-assessment tools and at-home health tests should not replace regular medical care.

Stroke

A stroke is a heart attack of the brain. It is the number one cause of severe, long-term disability.

High Stroke Risk Factors

High blood pressure

Diabetes

Heart disease (such as atrial fibrillation)

Previous stroke or transient ischemic attack

Cigarette smoking

Additional Risk Factors

Physical inactivity

Overweight or obesity

High cholesterol

Sickle cell disease

Drinking too much alcohol

A family history of stroke

Drug abuse

Genetic conditions, such as blood-clotting or vascular disorders (for example, Factor V Leiden or CADASIL)

Certain medications (such as hormonal birth control pills)

Being pregnant

Menopause

Stroke is an Emergency
Act Fast and Call 9-1-1

Few in the U.S. know the warning signs of stroke. Learning them – and acting FAST when they occur – could save one's life or the life of a loved one.

FACE: Ask the person to smile. Does one side of the face droop?

ARMS: Ask the person to raise both arms. Does one arm drift downward?

SPEECH: Ask the person to repeat a simple sentence. Does the statement sound slurred or strange?

TIME: Observing any of these signs (independently or together), call 9-1-1 immediately.

Stroke Prevention Guidelines

Know blood pressure (hypertension)

High blood pressure is a major stroke risk factor if left untreated. Have blood pressure checked yearly by a doctor or at health fairs, a local pharmacy or supermarket or with an automatic blood pressure machine.

Identify atrial fibrillation (Afib)

Afib is an abnormal heartbeat that can increase stroke risk by 500 percent. Afib can cause blood to pool in the heart and may form a clot and cause a stroke. A doctor must diagnose and treat Afib.

Stop Smoking

Smoking doubles the risk of stroke. It damages blood vessel walls, speeds up artery clogging, raises blood pressure and makes the heart work harder. Stopping smoking today will immediately begin to decrease risk.

Control of Alcohol Use

Based on studies drinking alcohol drinking cause strokes. Most doctors recommend not drinking or drinking only in moderation – no more than two drinks each day. Remember that alcohol can negatively interact with other drugs.

Act fast at the first warning sign of stroke. If one has any stroke symptoms, seek immediate medical attention.

Know Cholesterol Levels

Cholesterol is a fatty substance in the blood that is made by the body. It also comes in food. High cholesterol levels can clog arteries and cause a stroke. If total cholesterol level is more than 200, see a doctor.

Many people with diabetes have health problems that are also stroke risk factors. A doctor can prescribe a nutrition program, lifestyle changes and medicine to help control diabetes.

Manage Exercise and Diet

Excess weight strains the circulatory system. Exercise five times a week. Maintain a diet low in calories, salt, saturated and trans fats, and cholesterol. Eat five servings of fruits and vegetables daily.

Treat Circulation Problems

Fatty deposits can block arteries carrying blood to the brain and lead to a stroke. Seek if treatment for other problems such as sickle cell disease or severe anemia.

Chapter Key Takeaways

Take preventive steps.

Know the warning signs.

Call 9-1-1 immediately.

Take a baby aspirin.

The Church has a responsibility to provide life-stage lessons to assist with this vital life process.

Physical Health Exercise

Be Healthier & Happier

There are numerous reasons to exercise:

Alleviates anxiety

Boosts creative thinking, immune system, mental health, and productivity

Builds self-esteem

Decreases osteoporosis risk

Eases back pain

Fights dementia

Gives confidence

Has an anti-aging effect

Helps to control addictions, keep focus in life and self-control

Helps prevent strokes

Improves appetite, balance & coordination, body image, cholesterol levels, concentration, eating habits, learning abilities, joint function, quality of life, muscle strength, oxygen levels to cells, posture, skin tone & color, and sleeping patterns

Increases energy & endurance, longevity, pain resistance, sex drive & satisfaction, and sports performance

Keeps body fit & able and brain fit

Lessons fatigue

Lifts mood

Lowers risk of (certain) cancers, diabetes, and high blood pressure

Makes for feeling happier and life more exciting

Prevents colds and muscle loss

Reduces feelings of depression and stress

Sharpens memory

Strengthens Bones and Heart

There are several exercises to help with physical fitness for a healthier and happier life. The more common of these are bicycling, fishing, golfing, hiking, running, swimming and walking.

In this chapter, we will explore something that most of us can do: walking, which has enormous health benefits.

The Top Reasons to Walk

Walking prevents type 2 diabetes. The Diabetes Prevention Program showed that walking 150 minutes per week and losing just 7% of one's body weight (12-15 pounds) can reduce your risk of diabetes by 58%.

Walking strengthens the heart if a male. In one study, mortality rates among retired men who walked less than one mile per day were near twice that among those who walked more than two miles per day.

Walking strengthens the heart if a female. Women in the Nurse's Health Study (72,488 female nurses) who walked three hours or more per week reduced their risk of a heart attack or other coronary event by 35% compared with women who did not walk.

Walking is right for the brain. In a study on walking and cognitive function, researchers found that women who walked the equivalent of a leisurely pace at least 1.5 hours per week had significantly better cognitive function and less cognitive decline than women who walked less than 40 minutes per week. Think about that!

Walking is right for the bones. Research shows that postmenopausal women who walk approximately one mile each day have higher whole-body bone density than women who walk shorter distances, and walking is also useful in slowing the rate of bone loss from the legs.

Walking helps alleviate symptoms of depression. Walking for 30 minutes, three to five times per week for 12 weeks reduced symptoms of depression as measured with a standard depression questionnaire by 47%.

Walking reduces the risk of breast and colon cancer. Women who performed the equivalent of one hour and 15 minutes to two and a half hours per week of brisk walking had an 18% decreased risk of breast cancer compared with inactive women. Many studies have shown that exercise can prevent colon cancer, and even if a person develops colon cancer, the benefits of exercise appear to continue both by increasing quality of life and reducing mortality.

Walking improves fitness. Walking just three times a week for 30 minutes can significantly increase cardio respiratory fitness.

Walking in short bouts improves fitness, too! A study of sedentary women showed that short sessions of brisk walking (three 10-minute walks per day) resulted in similar improvements in fitness and were at least as effective in decreasing body fatness as long bouts (one 30-minute walk per day).

Walking improves physical function. Research shows that walking improves fitness and physical function and prevents physical disability in older persons.

Before presenting several walking tips, here are a few fun facts about walking:

Brisk walking helps reduce body fat, lower blood pressure, and increase high-density lipoprotein.

A former neon-sign salesman, Jean Beliveau walked the longest walk around the world. He walked 46,600 miles around 64 countries. The trip took him 11 years.

Race-walking has been an official Olympic sport for over 90 years. Distances vary from 1 mile to 95 miles. Race-walking usually is not the most popular sport in the Olympics.

The United States walks the least of any industrialized nation.

Typical pair of tennis shoes will last 500 miles of walking.

On average, a person would need to walk seven hours to burn off a Super-Sized Coke, fries, and a Big Mac.

Researchers note that the human backbone was not designed to work in the vertical position of walking on two legs. That is why modern humans suffer from sore backs, slipped discs, arthritis, and more.

Experts suggest walking 6,000 steps a day to improve health and 10,000 steps a day to lose weight.

A 150-pound woman would have to walk four mph for 48 minutes equivalent to just over 3 miles to burn off a 240-calorie donut. A 2000 study reported that walking regularly (three times or more a week for half an hour or more) saves $330 a year in health care costs.

Amish men take about 18,425 steps per day. Amish women take about 14,196. The average American adult takes about 4,000 steps per day. Only 4% of Amish are obese, compared to 31% of the general population.

The best way to lose weight by walking is to take a longer, moderately paced walk (40 minutes at 60-65% maximum heart rate). Shorter, faster steps (20-25 minutes at 75%-85% maximum heart rate) are best for conditioning the heart and lungs.

A significant difference between walking and running is the amount of time each foot contacts the ground. While walking, at least one foot is in contact with the ground at any given time, and the length of time the foot is in contact is more extended than while running. During a run, foot contact with the ground is less than walking, and there is a period where both feet are not in contact with the ground.

Walking can help decrease the risk of heart attack, lower the risk of developing type 2 diabetes, and can even reduce the risk of bone fracture. Additionally, brisk walking can reduce stress and depression levels, as well as improve cancer survival rates.

A person is 36 more times likely to be killed walking than by driving a car. A person is 300 times more likely to be killed walking than by flying in an airplane.

Even though Americans use walking as their mode of transportation in less than 6% of their trips, over 13% of all traffic deaths involve pedestrians.

The most popular form of exercise in the United States is walking.

Even though over 40% of the trips taken in the U.S. are less than one mile, less than 10% is by walking or biking.

In 1970, 66% of children walked to the school of all trips

Today, only 13% walk.

Less than 50% of American adults exercise enough to gain significant health or benefits. Inactivity is the second leading cause of preventable death in the U.S., second only to tobacco use.

Mortality rates among retired men who walked less than one mile per day were almost twice as much as those who walked more than 2 miles per day.

Researchers have found that women who walked at least 1.5 hours per week had significantly better cognitive function than women who walked less than 40 minutes a week.

Walking helps prevent osteoporosis. Research shows that postmenopausal women who walk around one mile per day each day have higher whole-body bone density than women who walk less.

Walking reduces the risk of both breast and colon cancer.

There are two types of regular walking: 1) power walking (or speed walking), and 2) race walking. Race walking is an Olympic sport with rules, while power walking is a recreational sport.

Experts note that when shopping for walking shoes, one should always buy shoes that feel comfortable right away. There is no "breaking-in period." Also, feet swell during the day, so it is important to get fitted for walking shoes at the end of the day when feet are their largest.

The average human walking speed is about 3.1 miles per hour.

Age of Walkers in the United States

Age	Percent
5-15	15.2%
16-24	9.3%
25-39	9.2%
40-64	7.8%
65 and over	6.9%

Research has shown that the benefits of walking and moderate physical activity for at least 30 minutes a day can help:

Reduce the risk of coronary heart disease

Improve blood pressure and blood sugar levels

Improve blood lipid profile

Maintain body weight and lower the risk of obesity

Enhance mental well-being

Reduce the risk of osteoporosis

Reduce the risk of breast and colon cancer

Reduce the risk of non-insulin dependent (type 2) diabetes

There are benefits of the above simple activities.

Waking Safety Tips

Keep safety in mind when planning the route and the time of the walk:

When walking at dawn, dusk, or night, wear a reflective vest or brightly colored clothing

Walk in a group when possible

Notify local police station of the group's walking time and route

Do not wear jewelry

Do not wear headphones

Be aware of surroundings.

Turn walking into a fitness stride requires good posture and purposeful movements. Ideally, here is how one looks when walking:

Head is up. Looking forward, not at the ground.

Your neck, shoulders, and back are relaxed, not stiffly upright.

Swing one's arms freely with a slight bend in the elbows. A little pumping with arms is OK.

Slightly tighten stomach muscles, and back is straight, not arched forward or backward.

Walk smoothly, roll foot from heel to toe.

When starting a walking routine, remember to:

Get the right gear. Choose shoes with proper arch support, a firm heel, and thick flexible soles to cushion feet and absorb shock. When walking outdoors when it is dark, wear bright colors or reflective tape for visibility.

Choose a course carefully. When walking outdoors, avoid paths with cracked sidewalks, potholes, low-hanging limbs or uneven turf.

Warm up. Stroll for five to 10 minutes to warm up muscles and prepare the body for exercise.

Cooldown. At the end of a walk, saunter for five to 10 minutes to help muscles cool down.

Stretch. After a cool down, gently stretch muscles. Remember to warm up first before walking.

Follow these additional walking safety tips:

Use closed toe, comfortable shoes that will not slip.

Consider wearing clothes that drivers can easily see. Light or bright colors, reflective material and flashing lights are best.

Choose a route with sidewalks or a shoulder to give one space away from traffic.

If there are no sidewalks, walk facing traffic.

Essential things to carry are water, a driver's license or ID, and a cell phone.

Always look for cars before crossing a street or stepping off a curb.

Use crosswalks and follow traffic signals when crossing at street lights

Always use sidewalks when they are available. If not, walk on the left side of the street, facing traffic.

Be predictable.

Before stepping in front of a car, make eye contact with the driver and plan on stopping and have time to stop.

Walk like drivers do not know the right-of-way walk rules.

Distracted walking can be deadly:

Unplug headphones when crossing the street.

Hang-up one's cell phones until out of the intersection

Texting can wait until one is safe.

Seasonal walking safety tips:

WINTER

Dress in layers to keep warm and dry.

Remember the hat and gloves.

Use shoes that will not slip on snow and ice. Ice grippers for the bottom of shoes can help avoid slipping.

Walk with hands out pockets for more balance.

SPRING

Check the weather and be prepared for sun, rain or even snow.

A hat, light jacket, and umbrella are useful items to carry for spring weather.

SUMMER

Drink water before walking and avoid alcohol and caffeinated drinks. Carry extra water to drink as walking.

Know the signs of heat sickness and seek shelter if symptoms are present.

Signs of heat sickness include:

Heavy sweating

Weakness

Muscle cramps

Dizziness

Headache

Nausea/vomiting

Fainting

FALL

Layer clothing for both warm and cold temperatures.

A hat, light jacket, and umbrella are useful items to carry for fall weather.

"We all need 30 minutes or more of physical activity most days of the week," says Julia Valentour, a personal trainer and program coordinator for the American Council on Exercise. "So when it is not practical to be walking outdoors, it is important to find creative ways to get moving inside."

Inviting a friend over and try the following 30-minute plan below to increase energy and keep off the pounds:

Indoor Walking Routine

Minutes	Moves
0:00-2:00	**Heel taps:** Alternate tapping right and left heels out in front.
2:01-4:00	**High knees:** Lift the right knee and raise both arms overhead. Continue alternating legs.
4:01-6:00	**Jumping jacks:** Keep it at a low intensity.
6:01-8:00	**Stairs:** Go up and down a flight of steps. No stairs, consider investing in an exercise step.
8:01-10:00	**Brisk walk:** Move around the house quickly, focusing on breathing.
10:01-12:00	**Squats:** Stand with legs shoulder-width apart (hold on to the back of a chair if necessary). Lower body, so thighs are parallel.
12:01-14:00	Brisk walk.
14:01-16:00	**Bird dogs:** Get on all fours with hands directly below the shoulders. Slowly raise and straighten the left leg out and the right arm forward, so both are parallel to the floor. Repeat with the opposite leg and arm.
16:01-18:00	Brisk walk.
18:01-20:00	**Glute bridge:** Lie on the back with knees bent and feet flat on the floor, hip-width apart. Gently contract glutes and raise hips, forming a straight line from the shoulders to

	knees. Lower and repeat.
20:01-22:00	Brisk walk.
22:01-24:00	**Plank:** Lie on the stomach. Lift the body into a push-up position (arms straight but not locked) while maintaining a straight line from head to toes. Avoid sagging the lower back, raising the hips, or bending the knees. Hold for 10-30 seconds. Lower and repeat.
24:01-26:00	Brisk walk.
26:01-30:00	Cool down with these three yoga poses. **Downward dog:** Get on all fours with palms flat on the floor, hands shoulder-width apart, and toes curled back. Lift your buttocks and straighten the legs. Relax the head and neck between the shoulders and attempt to put the heels flat on the floor. The body will form an inverted V. **Cobra:** From the previous position, lower onto the stomach, legs flat on the ground and toes pointed. Straighten arms and lift the chest away from the ground, so lower back is arched. **Child's pose:** End exercise by bringing the body to a kneeling position and sit on the feet, directed outward. Reach arms forward and place forehead on the floor.

Chapter Key Takeaways

Walking produces many health benefits.

Walking is simple to do.

Waking can be outdoors or indoors.

Walking can be alone or with another.

The Church has a responsibility to provide life-stage lessons to assist with this vital life process.

Physical Health Nutrition
God's Pharmacy

God first separated the salt water from the fresh, made dry land, planted a garden, made animals and fish, all before making a human. He created and provided what we would need before we were born.

Healthy lifestyle tips:

It starts with a well-balanced diet

Limit sodium intake. Eat less than 1500 mg/day - use low sodium or sodium-free spices instead of salt.

Limit saturated fat (butter, milk fats, high-fat cuts of meat). Replace saturated fats with mono and poly-unsaturated fats (soft margarine, canola and olive oil).

Eat the "rainbow." Include 2.5 cups of brightly-colored fruits and vegetables.

Choose about 5.5 oz. of lean protein. Proteins are in lean cuts of meat, poultry, seafood, and legumes. Limit eggs, nuts, and seeds consumed each week, due to high-fat content.

Make half one's grains whole grains. Aim for 6 oz. per day, with 3 oz. from whole grain sources that are high in B Vitamins, Iron, Magnesium, Selenium, and fiber.

Good health needs more than 40 different nutrients, and no one food supplies them all. Eat a balanced, healthy diet. Alegria Aigen, M.S., R.D., L.D.N., a registered dietitian at Hebrew Rehabilitation Center, offers the following tips:

Eat a variety of nutrient-rich foods daily.

Enjoy plenty of fruits and vegetables; five servings a day may help prevent cancer and reduce the risk for obesity, heart disease, and hypertension.

Focus on whole grains such as wheat bread and brown rice to provide one with fiber, which will help one, feel fuller for a more extended period of time. Fiber is also beneficial in controlling blood sugar.

Lean protein, such as chicken and fish, are high for muscle health.

Low-fat dairy products are beneficial for bone health, as they are rich in calcium and Vitamin D.

Maintain a healthy body weight; check with one's doctor or registered dietitian for a weight management plan.

Eat moderate portions, especially when dining out.

Eat regular meals; skipping meals can lead to overeating at the next meal.

Make diet changes gradually and set realistic goals.

Eating a well-balanced diet with variation and in moderation, with foods from all five major food groups (grains (whole), vegetables, fruits, milk & dairy, meat & beans), will provide most of the vitamins and minerals your body needs on a daily basis, says Ruth Silah-Aaron,

R.D., L.D.N., Clinical Nutrition Manager & Dining Services at Hebrew Rehabilitation Center. Multivitamins and minerals are not a substitute for a healthful, balanced diet, but rather a supplement that ensures one receiving the recommended daily allowance (RDA) of vitamins and minerals. Vitamin and mineral supplementation are for individuals whose diet is poor. When considering vitamins and minerals, discuss with one's Primary Care Physician (PCP) or your dietitian which vitamins/minerals you should take.

Vitamins and minerals are naturally occurring substances that are necessary for many of the body's processes.

Multivitamins/ minerals come in the form of a tablet (chewed or swallowed whole), a capsule or a liquid. Multivitamins can be either taken alone or in combination with minerals; usually ten vitamins and ten minerals or as a single vitamin or a mineral.

Multivitamins and minerals are no substitute for a healthful, balanced diet, but rather a supplement that ensures one receives the recommended daily allowance (RDA) of vitamins and minerals. Individuals with poor diets need vitamin and mineral supplements. When considering vitamins and minerals, discuss with one's Primary Care Physician (PCP) or dietitian which vitamins/minerals to take.

Use a primary, standard multivitamin/ mineral supplying no more than 100 percent of one's RDA. A multivitamin/mineral that provides more than 100 percent of the RDA, in some cases, may be harmful.

Calcium is a mineral in the body that makes up bones, keeps them active, and is essential for a healthy life. Most of the calcium in one's body is stored in the teeth and bones, while the rest (about 1%) in the blood and soft tissues.

Lack of enough calcium in one's diet, the body automatically takes the calcium it needs from the bones. Continued lack of calcium the bones become weak, which can lead to osteoporosis and fractures. Nutrition specialists at Hebrew Rehabilitation Center recommend the following ways to ensure receiving 1,000 to 1,500 mg of calcium daily:

Eat two to three daily servings of dairy products (preferably low-fat milk, cheese or yogurt), which contain the most available form of calcium in the food supply.

Eat green, leafy vegetables, which can also contribute to calcium requirement. Other sources of calcium include tofu and salmon and sardines, both with bones.

Choose calcium-fortified foods such as orange juice, cereals, and bread.

Take a calcium supplement if not eating two to three servings of dairy products daily. Calcium citrate is a preferred form of calcium because it is usually better absorbed by the body.

Take a calcium supplement in divided doses for better absorption.

Make sure the calcium supplement contains Vitamin D, which works with calcium to maintain healthy bones or take a Vitamin D supplement, say, Elizabeth (Lisa) J. Samuelson, Ph.D. Associate Scientist, Institute for Aging Research, Assistant Professor, Harvard Medical School.

Water, which makes up nearly 60 percent of the human body, is one of the essential nutrients the body needs to function correctly. Some of its functions in the body are to regulate body temperature, lubricate and cushion joints, provide moisture to the skin and other tissues, aid in the process of digestion, and eliminate waste.

Without proper fluid intake, the body becomes dehydrated. Untreated severe dehydration can lead to seizures, permanent brain damage, and even death. Signs of dehydration include thirst, dry mouth, headaches, and dark colored urine. Seniors, in particular, need to take special precautions because their thirst mechanism is not as sensitive as that of younger people. Griselda Kote, R.D., L.D.N., Clinical Dietitian at Hebrew Rehabilitation Center, recommends the following tips for getting enough fluid during the day:

Drink at least eight eight-ounce glasses of liquid every day. Modify the above based on specific medical conditions, exercise, or the environment.

Limit intake of alcoholic and caffeinated beverages and those with added sugars such as fruit drinks, sports drinks, soft drinks, and sodas. These types of beverages may increase fluid needs and also add unwanted calories to one's diet!

Incorporating other foods in the diet can help meet daily fluid needs, such as decaffeinated tea, low sodium soups, milk, fruits and vegetables such as celery, tomatoes, oranges, and melons.

Dispassionate with plain water? Kick the water by adding a wedge of lime or lemon!

Drink throughout the day, not only when thirsty

Carry a bottle of water at all times, especially outdoors for an extended period.

Drink water before, during, and after physical exercise to offset the fluid the body loses through perspiration.

Keep track of the fluid intake throughout the day to ensure staying adequately hydrated.

Chapter Key Takeaways

Drink eight glass of water a day.

Do not smoke.

Drink in moderation.

Limit meal intake.

Eat a balanced diet.

Eat blueberries and watermelon.

Avoid pickles, pizza, soft drinks, pastry, and a second glass wine.

The Church has a responsibility to provide life-stage lessons to assist with this vital life process.

Physical Health Frailty

"That is the way it is with people who had a good life: they wonder where it went," Käthe Crum.

We are most fortunate to be able to include Milton Crum's first-person experience in "I'm Frail," and "I'm Old" *essays*: http://thecsr.org/resource-directory/im-old-an-essay-on-aging-by-milton-crum/. At age 90, his perspective tells it like it is. His writing is a realistic but sad view of the fourth age and frail adults (85plus), the least researched of all the life stages.

Three years ago, I was writing "I'm Old." I was still driving, going shopping, walking half a mile with our dog across uneven terrain, climbing flights of stairs, and feeling pretty confident about my condition at 87. I still believed that my ailments, and to some extent my wife Käthe's, could be fixed by medical interventions.

In "I'm Old," I wrote, "I will probably not only accept death but welcome it if I no longer have significant   unfinished business that I am able to do." I also wrote, "We approach death, many of us prepare by narrowing and simplifying our lives."

Moving into an assisted living facility fifteen months ago with Käthe was a radical narrowing and simplifying of our lives. I can still do a little writing, but Käthe is my primary joy and reason to get up in the morning.

Now, after three more years of "age-related decline," I'm frail, and I've almost had enough. So I am calling this paper "I'm Frail."

Frailty

In *Rethinking Aging: Growing Old and Living Well in an Overtreated Society*, Nortin M. Hadler, M.D., sets out three markers of frailty: (1) loss of any notion of invincibility, (2) loss of possibility for a subsequent life stage, and (3) loss of ability to do things essential to one's care.1 The first two markers apply totally. (1) Rather than feeling invincible, I feel increasingly weak mentally and physically. (2) I know that frailty is my last life stage. I was given a useful and long lifetime, but I've spent almost all of it. (3) the third marker applies increasingly. I no longer drive, shopping is only by the Internet, my walking is measured in feet on even surfaces, and I do no meal preparation. Even with eleven hours in bed at night, trying to get as much good sleep as possible at my age, I feel tired all day. I can still take care of my personal hygiene, but that could also end if I don't die soon enough. My brain still functions, but my ability to read, comprehend, and write has slowed. I use no prescription medications except drops in my eyes to relieve ocular hypertension. My frailty seems to be primarily a product of old age.

For most people (as documented by Muriel R. Gillick, M.D.), including Käthe, "frailty" denotes an array of chronic physical and mental problems, which means that frailty is not treatable as a specific disease. These problems are often coupled with increased dependency on the primary activities of daily living (ADLs) required for personal care.2 In Käthe's case, we are dealing with diabetes, sleep apnea, chronic heart failure, seizures, constipation, dementia resulting from brain atrophy caused by 18 years of small bleeding strokes and one clot stroke and confinement to a wheelchair except for walks up to the 100 feet between our rooms with an aide, using a walker.

Thus, frailty usually comprises a group of distinct but interconnected "complex issues" and "comorbid diseases."3 These factors lead to progressive weakness, stress, and exhaustion.4 There are treatments for some of the causes of frailty, but "the ultimate course is a downward one."5

I have long said and hoped that I would die healthy, but I missed membership in that small minority. Käthe and I were assigned to the overwhelming majority that must endure a "phase of frailty" that might include dementia before we die.6

By reading and experience, I know about frailty. This is my definition. Frailty is a condition, sometimes lasting years that most old people endure before death, during which various ailments conspire to make death more attractive than life. For me, frailty has almost accomplished its goal, except for Käthe.

Käthe

The care provided and the life together made possible by our assisted living facility for Käthe and me during our 15 months in residence have been as good as possible, given our conditions. Nevertheless, virtually all the people, activities, and possessions that enriched our lives in former days have been taken away, except having each other and our days together.

So far, I have been permitted by the facility, and I am still able to be Käthe's primary caretaker from arising to going to bed (each with a kiss) for transfers, exercising, and entertainment, making much use of the Internet. Käthe tells me that she is happy in this situation, and she seems to be. She once told me that she did not like receiving care from the staff because it makes her feel too dependent, but she added, "I don't mind being dependent on you because I love you and you love me."

We have talked about longevity having lost the attraction it once had and about our dread of being left alone and how life would not be worth living.

Käthe's ability to articulate her thoughts is limited, but she expresses her feelings. Asked about life without Milton, she says, "I wouldn't want to live if I could help it." I feel the same way about life without Käthe.

Without the present arrangement with Käthe, I would be hard pressed to find sufficient reasons to get up in the morning. Even with Käthe, I have begun to feel that I've almost had enough living without the people, possessions, and activities that once comprised my life.7 No matter what anyone does, from now on its downhill toward death.

We are both in what our final stage is and what it is to be hoped the shortest.

A Day of Frailty

Up at 6:30am, an exercise in an attempt to maintain some strength. 7:15am, walk 100 feet' to Käthe's room for a good morning kiss, after which she gets a snooze. I have coffee and newspaper before helping Käthe get up and dressed: helping with transfers from bed to walker to the toilet, a little washing up and getting dressed, transfer from toilet to walker, walk across the room to a wheelchair. With the help of an aide, Käthe usually gets a pre-breakfast 100 feet' walk. Her diabetic procedures and breakfast come. Käthe's upper-body exercises come next to my room, accompanied by music from the Internet.

After that, it's back to her room for brushing teeth and a 90-minute nap. 11:30am repeats much of Käthe's getting up, plus a few leg exercises and the diabetic procedures before lunch.

After lunch, in my room until another walk for Käthe before her 2:00pm nap. For entertainment, we use Internet radio or YouTube, sing children's or love songs, work together on a six-piece jigsaw puzzle, or talk. After the nap, another walk and time in my room for tea, crackers, and music before the diabetic procedures and supper. After supper, it's a shower for Käthe in two evenings. The other evenings we spend time in my room enjoying something on the Internet until getting ready for bed. Käthe's bedtime is about 6:30pm; mine is as soon after as I can make it.

During Käthe's nap times, I do my personal hygiene, place orders, pay bills, check finances, and write things like this. The days go by quickly; I don't have time on my hands.

This is a life radically narrowed and simplified compared to what it was even two years ago. The surprise is that we don't feel stir-crazy. It's because frailty down-sizes everything about us: our energy, our brains, our interests. We remember and are saddened by the loss of earlier activities, possessions, and contacts, but we accept their demise. We enjoy family visits, and knowing they are there provides an invaluable assurance, but we don't yearn to see them every day. Going to an excellent restaurant has lost its appeal. Käthe's brain seems to have lost its ability for culinary discrimination, and I no longer hunger for excellent food.

Life as a frail person is vastly different from life as being merely old: a transformation that can happen quickly or gradually.8

Death

We have long anticipated death in a rational way by making end-of-life arrangements, executing documents, and writing guides to help our survivors do the many things that survivors need to do. But now that the conspiracy of old age and ailments has wrought us frail, death has taken on a new reality; it's at the door. Neither our assisted living facility nor our doctors can restore us to a pre-frailty condition. At best, they can make the time between now and death as pleasant as possible. I hope that the assisted living facility will not think it their duty to take away whatever pleasures we still enjoy in an attempt to prolong our lives. And I hope that our families or our doctors will not feel obligated to stretch out our lives.

Most of the age 85plus interviewees in *Life Beyond 85 Years* did not fear death, but nearly all dreaded a long process of dying. One woman said, "Living this long is pure hell. The hardest thing I face has to be going on living." Käthe and I both hope that we will not be like this person and have people making efforts to extend our misery, perhaps assuming (without ascertaining what we want) that they are doing us a favor.9

As of this writing, life cannot be described as "pure hell," but we would not have chosen our present situation except by necessity. And we see other residents in conditions that, to us, fit the "pure hell" description.

Facing our Death

In his *How We Die*, Dr. Nuland lays out two options as we face our death. One is to battle death using all the weapons of "high-tech biomedicine." The other option is to acquiesce to death's power consciously.10 We are choosing the second option. In this choice, we are with the majority in *Older Adults' Views on Death*, a study based on interviews with people in the 70-97 age range, with a mean age of 80.7. About half the people chose to do nothing except live day by day until death comes naturally without medical or other intervention designed to prolong life. This choice was coupled with a desire to receive palliative care if needed. We both concur with this choice.11

Even when it's possible to postpone death, doing so often afflicts the frail person with "prolonged sickness, dependence, pain, and suffering."12

Postponing death is also costly in dollars. One out of every four Medicare dollars is spent on the frail in their last year of life in attempts to postpone death.13 Dr. Hadler warns against the tendency to mediatize and over treat the frail.14

There are two Greek words for "life." "Bios" denotes biological life; "zóé" denotes real and genuine life.15 We choose not to extend bios after frailty precludes zóé. It would be nice to have other choices, such as again living robustly in Alpine Lake in West Virginia, where we enjoyed twenty glorious retirement years. As goes the song, "Those were the days, my friend. We thought they'd never end. We'd sing and dance forever and a day. We'd live the life we choose. We'd fight and never lose, for we were young and sure to have our way." As the song goes, "Those were the days, my friend, we thought they'd never end," but they did.16 As I was writing these words, Käthe joined me in singing them. She then mused, "That's the way it is with people who had a good life: they wonder where it went."

Detente with Death

In his *Rethinking Aging: Growing Old and Living Well in an Overtreated Society*, Nortin Hadler, M.D., describes the unreality of trying to cure ailments in the 9th decade (Käthe is not there chronologically, but she is there functionally.). In Dr. Hadler's judgment, it makes no sense to cure the diseases one will die from within the ninth decade and little sense to cure the diseases that one will die from in the ninth decade if another is to take its place in short order.17

For all ages, there is evidence that attempts to cure can do more harm than good and the procedures can inflict misery.18 A Newsweek article, "One Word Can Save Your Life: No!", found that "more health care often means worse health."19

What all of us face is described by Dr. Sherwin Nuland in his *The Art of Aging*: a lifelong process in which "a healthy individual gradually deteriorates into one that is fraily vulnerable to disease and ultimate death."20 In his *How We Die*, Dr. Nuland argues that many people die of "old age," even though doctors are required to name some disease as the cause.21

Taking it as it Comes

A 100-year-old friend often advised, "You've got to take it as it comes." This is what he did, and it's what we are increasingly doing. Battling death requires exceptional effort and perseverance, and whatever life extension is won may be less attractive than death.

By choice or necessity, we have already reduced possible medical care and ceased some of our own efforts to postpone death. No longer do we eat only whole grain and the leanest meat; no longer do we drink only skim milk. I have skipped the five-year blood work and checking moles. I sometimes feel like my whole system is about to conk out, a feeling for which I would have seen a doctor in the past. Now, I take it as a possible quick way to die without a lengthy fearful process. With the concurrence of all three daughters, we have canceled appointments with Käthe's cardiologist. Käthe was first sent to a cardiologist several years ago by our primary care physician to get her blood pressure under control, and that has been done.

We also canceled a check of Käthe's Pacemaker because what the Pacemaker technician had told me about the low risk of malfunction seemed less than the risk of transporting Käthe in midwinter.

When Käthe had her first seizure, she was sent by ambulance to the ER, where she underwent the usual round of tests and there an attempt to have her see a neurologist, which we declined. There have been three more seizures in which Käthe was merely placed in her bed for rest and recovery. It is not clear whether or not permanent damage was done, but it does not seem that another visit to the ER would have helped. If in spite of our wishes not to, we get as far as the ER or ICU, we have made legal decisions by executing Do Not Resuscitate (DNR) forms, Physician Orders for Life-Sustaining Treatment (POLST) forms, Living Wills, and Medical Powers of Attorney for each of us.

I think that what we want for our time left is called "palliative care." The basic philosophy of palliative care is to achieve the best quality of life for patients, even when their illness cannot be cured.22 Palliative care is done by "relieving or soothing the symptoms of a disease or disorder without effecting a cure."23

Another factor is Käthe's multiple illnesses (multi-morbidity) situation, a condition shared by about 75% of people over 65, probably more at our ages. I might find multi-morbidity in me, too, if I had a physical exam. My blood pressure runs about 30 points higher than it used to, but I have arrived at a point where I am more interested in a good way to die than I am about treatments to extend life.

Johns Hopkins Medicine points out that treating each illness as if it stood alone can be detrimental.24 For anyone thinking about the multi-morbidity factor, the "Guiding Principles for the Care of Older Adults with Multi-morbidity Pocket Card" from The American Geriatrics Society might be useful.25

Religion and Faith

I have long since resonated with Karl Barth's dictum that "religion is the enemy of faith."26 Except for attending Sunday worship with Käthe at the National Cathedral via their website, religious practices are not playing a role in my life. However, several faith affirmations and images are operative for me. Most of them are contained in three items written by me, available on the Internet:

"Self-esteem/OKness: a personal story" online at http://www.ahpcc.org.uk/pdf/selfesteem.pdf

"Enduring Significance in My Faith" online athttp://www.ahpcc.org.uk/pdf/enduring.pdf or search http://books.google.com for "Enduring Significance in My Faith" to bring up a link to it as found in Robert W. Chism, *Longevity Response-Ability.*

Evil, Anger, and God. Go to http://books.google.com and search for 'Milton Crum Evil, Anger, and God'.

Walking through the "valley of the shadow of death," it is the evil of extended frailty that I fear more than death. (Psalm 23:4)

What's Next?

The odds are for a "progressive terminal decline" with constant fatigue, more sleep, and increased detachment from people, things, and activities until we die.27

Both of us have executed POLSTs, Living Wills, and Medical Powers of Attorney, and they are on file with the assisted living facility and our primary care physician, who works for our local hospital. Our concern about what's next related to the possible time between when we become too frail to continue our present lifestyle and before we are clearly terminally ill and the end-of-life directives become applicable.

With our assisted living facility, it's so far, so good. What's next, I am pondering. The way I imagine what's next is based partly on written descriptions of the likely future for us between

146

now and our deaths, such as those I have cited. My imagining is also based on the care of old people (sometimes including Käthe and me) that I have observed over the years in three different states in churches and commercial care facilities. Some of these memories include the following:

Disturbing Memories

There was an ancient invalid woman in our church who often said that she was tired of living and wanted to die. None of us took her seriously because none of us understood old age well enough to comprehend that she might have been totally serious. My seminary training included nothing about ministering to what Dr. Gillick calls the "frail elderly."[28]

I recall Sally, whose greatest pleasure seemed to be hot chocolate, but it was ordered that she got no hot chocolate unless she ate more. On one visit, I heard an aide telling Sally that she must eat before she could leave the table. When Sally protested, the aide argued that the food was good for her and that it would make her healthy. She asked the aide, "Why are you so mean to me?"

Did anyone ever ask Sally whether or not she would have chosen to live longer eating and drinking "right" or die sooner eating and drinking whatever she wanted? Did anyone listen to her wishes about her life and death?

I hope that as a 90-year-old, I will not suffer being patronized as a child. I hope the same for Käthe. There was a time in the past when she was so treated by a staff's comments about what she was eating. Käthe said, "It made me feel like a child. It made me feel dumb."

I would hope that Käthe and I will not be deprived of any pleasures we have left, even if the depriver's intention is to extend our lives. 29 What's a name for making somebody live against her/his wishes? In another place, there was an 85plus man who ate every bite of the high-calorie servings given him, and I saw him develop a Santa Claus stomach. So it seemed permissible to shorten one's life by overeating.

I am thinking about frail people whom I have seen put on oxygen or nebulizers. Was it for palliation or trying to postpone the death of people whose lives were limited to sleeping, being cleaned up, and eating?

Reassuring Memories

Regarding our desire for palliative care without heroic measures, I am thinking of people about whose last days I had some knowledge.

One person was very frail on arrival at a facility and was confined to her room, where she died after some weeks. There were no heroic medical interventions.

Another person had a fall and was placed in a nursing care facility, where he died sometime later. Again, I heard of no heroic attempts to prolong his life.

A 90plus friend was sent to the hospital with pneumonia. He was offered a radical intervention that might extend his life. He declined. It was as if he had read Dr. Hadler's warning cited above.

When I first met this person, he was walking well with a walker and eating heartily. He went downhill rapidly until he died from heart failure. He was given morphine at the end, but I think there were no heroic medical interventions.

The most we can hope for as our frailty compounds are that our care will contribute to the primary goal for Käthe and me, namely, maximizing pleasure and minimizing suffering with no illusion of curing either of us and with the recognition that our decrepitude will inevitably increase.

Discussion and Decision

Recognizing that the present life that we find worth living will end and will likely end while we are still alive came as a call to discussion and decision.

Käthe, two daughters who live nearby, and I began conversations about what kind of care we hoped for from our assisted living facility and our physician. Readings such as those cited above helped us analyze our situation and project likely futures.

We agreed on the following letter to the assisted living facility owners and staff, which includes registered nurses and our physician. We thought such a letter important because doctors and nurses are trained for and in their practice focus on fighting disease and extending life. It is reportedly difficult for some of them to shift focus from extending life to palliative care.30

Letter sent to Assisted Living Facility and Primary Care Physician

We're writing this letter in response to Milton and Käthe's wishes that their desires regarding life-extending care be clearly communicated and understood by all of us. We've had recent conversations with Käthe and Milton regarding their strong wishes regarding refusal of life-extending care.

As you know, both Käthe and Milton have executed POLST forms, Living Wills, and Medical Powers of Attorney. They are on file with Facility Name and Primary Care Physician. Käthe and Milton's present concerns have to do with the possibility that one of them may have an illness, complications, etc. before they are clearly terminal and their end-of-life directives become applicable.

They describe their present conditions as allowing for a 'worth-living quality of life,' but are clear that much-increased frailty, disability, or illness would result in a 'not-worth living quality of life.' And they have independently expressed their desire that the focus of their care is palliative rather than life-extending.

We are writing this to you because we want you to know their desires, and Heather, Cindy and Suzanne's support of Käthe and Milton's desires, as well as to assist in freeing you from legal or moral obligations to do everything possible to make Käthe and Milton live longer. Käthe and Milton both value the quality of life more than the length of life, and without sufficient quality, they do not want to live longer.

Some specific wishes and choices from Käthe and Milton follow:

Honor our right to refuse treatment.

Do whatever is needed to alleviate pain, even if it hastens death.

Do not administer oxygen or a nebulizer unless they can relieve suffering.

Allow us to determine what or how much we eat or drink.

Do not feed us things like Ensure or Mighty Shakes as a way of extending life.

Do not call an ambulance and send to ER or ICU.

Heather, Suzanne, and Cindy are supportive of Käthe and Milton's wishes regarding the above specifics. If you would like to meet with us to discuss further, we are readily available to get together. Thanks for the care.

Appreciatively, signed by Käthe and Milton Crum and three daughters

Epilogue

I have read this paper to Käthe. She found it "realistic" but "sad." Asked if things could be different, she said, "Not without a miracle, but that is unlikely." I agree. At one point, Käthe asked that we not read anymore because it was "too emotional." We took a break.

I'm Fail will probably be my last writing about old age. I hope that families of old people, as well as the doctors, nurses, and aides who care for them, will listen to the old people themselves about their choice between life-extending care and palliative care. Listening sometimes requires patience and alertness for non-verbal communication. It also requires laying aside the assumption that everyone wants to be kept alive regardless of the quality of life. However, the book *Older Adults' Views on Death* illustrates that their views can be elicited.

Notes

1. Nortin M. Hadler, *Rethinking Aging: Growing Old and Living Well in an Overtreated Society* (University of North Carolina, 2011), 159-160.

2. Muriel R. Gillick, M.D., *Lifelines: Living Longer, Growing Frail, Taking Heart* (Norton, 2001), x, xv-xvi, 5-6.

3. "diseases in addition to the primary disease."

4. Patricia M. Burbank, ed., Vulnerable Older Adults: Health Care Needs and Interventions (Springer, 2006), 25-26.

5. Victor G. Cicirelli, *Older Adults' Views on Death* (Springer, 2002), p. 4.

6. Muriel R. Gillick M.D., *Choosing Medical Care in Old Age: What Kind, How Much, When to Stop* (Harvard, 1998), 189.

7. An exercise used to simulate old age is to divide fifteen slips of paper into three groups

on which to write (1) your most important people, (2) your most enjoyable activities, and (3) your most treasured possessions. One-by-one, the slips are taken away.

8. Muriel R. Gillick, M. D., Lifelines: *Living Longer, Growing Frail, Taking Heart* (Norton, 2001), 5-6.

9. Colleen Johnson and Barbara M. Barer, Life *Beyond 85 Years* (2003), 202-206, 208.

10. Sherwin B. Nuland, *How We Die* (1995), 10.

11. Victor G. Cicirelli, *Older Adults' Views on Death* (Springer, 2002), 6-7, 9, 12, 32.

12. Patricia M. Burbank, ed., *Vulnerable Older Adults: Health Care Needs and Interventions* (Springer, 2006), 9.

13. Penelope Wang, "Cutting the high cost of end-of-life care" (CNN Money, 2012).

14. Nortin M. Hadler, *Rethinking Aging: Growing Old and Living Well in an Overtreated Society* (University of North Carolina, 2011) 1, 3.

15. Strong's Concordance http://biblehub.com/greek/979.htm and Thayer's Greek Lexicon, http://biblehub.com/thayers/2222.htm.

16. From the song used in movies, TV, and often recorded in many languages. See http://en.wikipedia.org/wiki/Those_Were_the_Days_ (song).

17. Nortin M. Hadler, *Rethinking Aging: Growing Old and Living Well in an Overtreated*

Society (University of North Carolina, 2011), 175-176.

18. Penelope Wang, "Cutting the high cost of end-of-life care" (CNN Money, 2012).

19. "One Word Can Save Your Life: No!" Newsweek, August 14, 2011. http://www.thedailybeast.com/newsweek/2011/08/14/some-medical-tests-procedures-domore-harm-than-good.html.

20. Sherwin B. Nuland, *The Art of Aging: A Doctor's Prescription for Well-Being* (2008), 27-28, 59.

21. Sherwin B. Nuland, *How We Die* (1995), 43-44, 72.

22. Stephanie C. Paulus, "Palliative Care: An Ethical Obligation" (Mark Kula Center for Applied Ethics, Santa Clara University, 2008). http://www.scu.edu/ethics/practicing/focusareas/medical/palliative.html.

23. http://www.thefreedictionary.com/palliative

24. http://www.hopkinsmedicine.org/geriatric_medicine_gerontology/aging_research/health_services_research/multimorbidity.html

25. "Guiding Principles for the Care of Older Adults with Multi-morbidity Pocket Card" from The American Geriatrics Society. http://www.americangeriatrics.org/files/documents/MultimorbidityPocketCardPrintable.pdf

26. Quoted in Boston Collaborative Encyclopedia of Western Theology, http://people.bu.edu/wwildman/bce/barth.htm.

27. Colleen Johnson and Barbara M. Barer, *Life Beyond 85 Years* (2003), 207.

28. Muriel R. Gillick M.D., *Choosing Medical Care in Old Age: What Kind, How Much, When to Stop* (Harvard, 1998).

29. In the 1990 case of Nancy Beth Cruzan before United States Supreme Court, "the majority assumed   that the United States Constitution would grant a competent person a constitutionally protected right to refuse lifesaving hydration and nutrition." Annette Clark, "The Right to Die: The Broken Road from Quinlan to Schiavo" in the Loyola University Chicago Law Journal, Vol 37 (2006), 394. Online at http://www.luc.edu/media/lucedu/law/students/publications/llj/pdfs/clark.pdf

30. Virginia Morris, *Talking About Death* (Algonquin Books, 2004), 245-247.

Religious Health Ageism

Challenging Discrimination

This chapter has information from the Gray Panthers (Age and Young in Action).

Ageism Defined

Ageism is arbitrary discrimination based on chronological age. Ageism is as severe and pervasive as racism and sexism. Ageism is harmful to all age groups and oppresses both the old and the young. It deprives both groups of power and status and the right to control their own lives and destinies.

The greatest handicap associated with old age is the ageist barriers and prejudices imposed on the old by society's orientation to youth. We have been conditioned to despise and devalue our own experiences, skills, gray hair and wrinkles. This thinking has so brainwashed many that we rarely admit our real age and try to keep alive the youth cult by lies, self-deception and futile efforts to look young.

The subject of age affects all persons: we are becoming older. Powerlessness and alienation affect young as well as old in destructive ways.

Examples of Ageism

Social Security

Black balloon birthday parties

"You do not look 40" - or whatever age

Limited positive roles in TV and movies for older people

Lower ticket costs for older adults for movies

Seating old people away from the active, entry area in a restaurant

Not being waited on in line/getting passed by for others who came later

"Terrible twos" used to describe a vital life stage of growing independence

Dreading being a parent of teenagers

People in their twenties being told they are too young to work with "senior citizens."

Lying about one's age for fear of negative perceptions, treatment, or eligible for some benefit

The absence of older models in advertising (clothing, cars)

Lack of old people in a position of influence, decision-making

Efforts to create sub-minimum wage for teen jobs

The assumption that young people are computer whizzes and older people are computer-phobic

The stereotype that youths are drug addicts or gang members Cosmetics focused on anti-aging

Parallel Myths of Youth & Elders

Deemed too young or too old to contribute

Take too many drugs

Are unproductive

Should not/can not have sex

Do not have money

Do not know what they are talking about (so can be discounted)

Want to be left alone or only want to be with "own kind."

Other Myths About Aging

Older adults are less attractive.

Losing memory is a normal part of growing old

Mental ability declines with age

Old people are physically unable to function

Aging is terrible

Old people are bored

Creating an Age-Integrated Society

What is meant by the phrase "age-integrated society"? It may be defined as one in which the designation and identification of age groups—youth, middle-age, old-age – serve to bring those of different ages together to the maximum feasible extent. In other words, any awareness of differences among age groups leads to "age appropriateness" in services and group relations. In addition, an age-integrated society is one in which:

There is an atmosphere that supports intergenerational contact and unity, as well as genuine economic independence for all age groups. National policies do not segregate or stigmatize people as a result of their age and do not place them independent and depersonalized positions. Social policy-making is shared among all age groups. Social status is not based on chronological age. National policy honors the social contract between generations.

Mandatory retirement by our government is the single most discriminating law ever written. It removes the ability to work; creates fear and want; destroys the American work ethic, worker purpose, stability, pride, satisfaction, discipline, independence; reduces the workforce of capable employees and makes workers more dependent on the government.

Chapter Key Takeaways

"We need to become pro-aging and embrace the opportunities that aging provides," Jamie Lee Curtis Do not lie about your age

Let your hair be its natural color

Quit complimenting people on how young they look

Write to your local news media when a headline or cartoon is ageist

Monitor advertising—write complaints, boycott products/places

Voice your objections

Educate others

Challenge stereotypes about age

Refuse to buy derogatory birthday cards

Research, monitor, and question the responsiveness of institutions to age

Get to know people across age boundaries

Don't patronize people who are old

Don't mix illness with aging

Be aware of the language that is stereotyping

Don't tell jokes that make fun of growing old

Challenge ageism

The Church has a responsibility to provide life-stage lessons to assist with this vital life process.

Religious Health Entitlement

"Whatever you do, work at it with all your heart, as working for the Lord, not for human masters, since you know that you will receive an inheritance from the Lord as a reward. It is the Lord Christ one are serving,"
Colossians 3:23–24 (NIV).

A government big enough to give all one wants is big enough to take all one has."

—President Gerald Ford

"The problem with socialism is that you eventually run out of other people's money."

—Margaret Thatcher

"I cannot undertake to lay my finger on that article of the Constitution which granted a right to Congress of expending, on objects of benevolence, the money of their constituents."

—James Madison

"You cannot help people permanently by doing for them, what they could and should do for themselves."

—Abraham Lincoln

"As parents, we owe our children food, clothing, health care and shelter, not fun with friends, designer clothing, cell phones with data plans, a car or a party-school college experience." If kids want those things, they need to earn it for themselves. Otherwise, they feel entitled instead of appreciative."

—Ellie Kay, family finance expert

This chapter has information from Pastor Bruce Goettsche's sermon on July 29, 2007, entitled "Overcoming the Obstacles of Life" (www.union church.com).

The American Dream does not come from a government paycheck. However, there are more government checks issued for entitlement than paychecks issued by American businesses. By 2030, entitlements plus interest will exceed total revenue.

In the Declaration of Independence, we find these words: "We hold these truths to be self-evident, that all men are created equal, that they are endowed by their Creator with certain unalienable Rights, that among these are Life, Liberty and the pursuit of Happiness, --That to secure these rights, Governments are instituted among Men, deriving their just powers from the consent of the governed."

The "certain unalienable Rights" that are mentioned are "Life, Liberty and the pursuit of Happiness." It is sad indeed that we have drifted so far from our founding and the Bible, that many of our citizens have developed an "Entitlement Mentality." Actually, there are illegal aliens within our borders who are very aware of this "Entitlement Mentality." The cold, hard fact is that this "Entitlement Mentality" is actually being advertised nationally. Folks are being taught how to get things from the government. Many promises made during the presidential race were directed toward this so-called "right." Promises were made concerning health care, housing, higher education, and even the redistribution of wealth from the haves to the have nots. The prize goes to the person making the most promises regarding these "Entitlements." We have become a "Welfare State," yet we do not fare well.

The U.S. Constitution, Article. IV, Section 2, is the only use of the word "entitled" referring to individuals. It states, "The Citizens of each State shall be entitled to all privileges and Immunities of Citizens in the several states." The other 3 times refer to the states. The Bill of Rights as well grants nothing in the way of entitlements." Our Nation's motto is "In God We Trust," yet it is a reality that many people have a new motto, namely, "In Government We Trust."

Combating the Sense of Entitlement

So how do we combat this rampant mentality in our society? Here are some simple principles.

We must understand that some people do need help. Yes, there are many lazy people in the world. There will always be people who feel the world owes them something. However, there are times when people need real help and cannot do for themselves. Our job is to help these people in any way that we can.

We must face the facts. Life as we know it is not fair. Some people seem to have it easier than others, and none knows why. God does not treat everyone the same. He raises some up and not others. One is not entitled to what everyone else has! God does not owe one anything! On the contrary, we owe Him everything. We must stop playing the part of a victim!

We must change our work ethic. People used to talk about the Protestant work ethic. It was an attitude that believed that God had placed us where we are in the world so that we can honor and glorify Him. No matter what the job, we work at it with all our heart as to the Lord. Work is not a necessary evil; it is our mission field.

We must adjust our focus:

We should focus on being like Jesus rather than the "successful people" of our world. He is our goal, not the man in the smile and $1000 suit.

We should focus on what we can do for others instead of what others can do for us.

We should focus on helping people to manage on their own rather than merely throwing money at them.

We should measure ourselves by the Word of God rather than measuring the Word of God by our thoughts and desires.

Chapter Lesson Brief

Cultivate an attitude of gratitude. Start each day thanking God for all that He has given: a new day of life; His mercy and grace; family; health; His promises in the Word of God; a purpose in living. Be specific. Look for opportunities to thank people for their work and the blessings they have given.

Make a conscious effort to look for ways that can give to others rather than focusing on what one thinks one deserves from others.

Count the number of "whiners" you encounter in a day. Notice the sense of entitlement they have and determine to be different.

Work on growing a relationship with God. Practice spiritual discipline. Make time to read the Word. Work at prayer. Be good stewards of what one has. Read a challenging Christian book stop demanding to be spoon fed.

Be accountable. When hearing one say or thinking about what one "deserve," stop and ask yourself why you think you "deserve" these things.

Work to build responsibility into one's children. Help them to understand that the world does not revolve around them now so that they will not be shocked when it does not revolve around them later.

Diligently pursue contentment. Learn to receive what God has given to one gladly. Enjoy life as it is rather than longing for a day when things will be better.

Chapter Key Takeaway

We may never change that attitude of entitlement that people seem to have, but we can change our attitude. We can choose to focus on what a gracious God has given us. We can diligently pursue humility, holiness, and service. We can learn to be content, and we can learn to be thankful. We can learn to be givers rather than takers. Moreover, if we do this, our relationship with God and with others' will be enriched.

The Church has a responsibility to provide life-stage lessons to assist with this vital life process.

Religious Health Materialism

"Whatever you do, work at it with all your heart, as working for the Lord, not for human masters, since you know that you will receive an inheritance from the Lord as a reward. It is the Lord Christ one is serving,"
Colossians 3:23–24 (NIV)."

This chapter has information from a sermon by Pastor Dr. Tim Smith entitled "Confronting Culture – Materialism," at Gretna United Methodist Church in 2011.

When it comes to materialism, has any nation ever surpassed what we are seeing in the United States right now? We define our lives by how much stuff we have, social status by how much money we make, what we own and wear and where we live. Even most of the important dates on our calendar are all about materialism. Even the phrase "the American Dream" speaks more about owning a house, a car, vacations, retirement rather than freedom and pursuing your dream and potential. Shopping malls are our churches, celebrities our gods, and "People" and "Vogue" our Bibles. Like Paris Hilton and Kim Kardashian, one can be famous just by being rich.

We have become a secular nation, and we know it. According to American Mythos, a national survey showed that 82% of Americans thought they were materialistic and 77% said they are self-indulgent.

What exactly is materialism? It is "a preoccupation with possessions and believing that products bring happiness and success."

Why have we become so materialistic?

UNHAPPINESS: Americans as a whole are unhappy. Americans take more anti-depressants than anyone else on the planet. When people are unhappy, they turn to material things to feel better.

LONELINESS: We are an incredibly single nation. Today, the United States has the highest percentage of one-person households on the entire globe. We do not even know the people who live next door to us. Faith Popcorn noted two decades ago that we go from work to home and stay there without connecting to friends or neighbors as in times past. She called this cocooning. Moreover, though we have more technology than ever before to keep us connected, those interactions are superficial at best, leaving us longing for true emotional intimacy with others.

ADVERTISING: Susannah Opree writes, "It is really about the way that advertising tries to sell products. The message is: 'Buy this product because it will make you happy or make you more popular.'"

PEER PRESSURE: One's friends and family buy a new product and tell one how great it is, and sooner or later one begins to think one needs it, too. Add to that peer pressure and the "Keeping up with the Joneses" syndrome, and others play a significant role in our lives when it comes to materialism.

What the Bible says about materialism:

We are blessed to be a blessing.

"Do not store up for yourselves treasures on Earth, where moth and rust destroy, and where thieves break in and steal. However, store up to one's treasures in Heaven, where moth and rust do not destroy, and where thieves do not break in and steal. For where one's treasure is, there one's heart will also be," Matthew 6:19-21 (NIV).

There is only one God. "No one can serve two masters. Either he will hate the one and love the other, or he will be devoted to the one and despise the other. One cannot serve both God and money," Matthew 6:24 (NIV). "You shall have no other gods before me," Exodus 20:3 (NIV)

It causes trouble and problems in a person's life. "For the love of money is a root of all kinds of evil. Some people, eager for money, have wandered from the faith and pierced themselves with many grief's," I Timothy 6:10. Materialism not only impacts the lives we lead but also what type of people we become. Materialistic people tend to be narcissistic and concerned with impressing people. They tend to be anxious, depressed, and have low self-esteem. Their peers are less like them. They have relatively poor relationship skills and lower quality relationships that are less satisfying and become less satisfied with their lives in general over time. As a result, they incur many mental health costs and are more prone to depression.

Sadly, no matter how big our homes are or how many shiny new toys we accumulate, we never seem to be happy. We always want more, and we always seem to be willing to go into more debt to get it. We have accumulated the biggest mountain of debt in the history of the world. More things do not equal happiness. Unfortunately, most Americans have bought into this lie, believing that more equals a better and happier life. We have more "stuff" than any other society in the history of the world, but it has not made us happy. Ed Diener, a University of Illinois psychology professor and happiness expert, says that materialism becomes "a more difficult goal than many because it is open-ended and goes on forever - we can always want more, which is usually not true of other goals, such as friendship.

Children who were less satisfied with their lives become more materialistic over time when frequently exposed to advertising that teaches them that possessions are a way to increase happiness. The average American child is exposed to 40,000 commercials annually, all with the same message: buy this, and one will be happy! Materialism only grows when they become teens. Teens not only want the latest games and clothes but also think owning these things will bring them happiness, friends, and popularity. Teens spend $28 billion a year on themselves, not including the more than $200 billion their parents spend on them.

Materialism impacts marriages, too. Researchers found that couples in which one or both partners placed a high priority on getting or spending money were much less likely to have satisfying and stable marriages. Jason Carroll, a BYU professor of family life in Provo, Utah, says, "Materialism characteristics are less effective communication, higher levels of negative conflict, lower relationship satisfaction, and less marriage stability."

Moreover, men, it is not the woman's fault! Men will argue that women are more materialistic, citing the commonly held notion that women tend to look for partners that have significant wealth, as well as women's shopping habits and concern for clothing, shoes, purses, jewelry, make-up, polished nails, cell phones, perfume, hair. However, men are just as guilty, and some of the research shows that men are just as greedy if not more as their female counterparts. Just look at men's preoccupation with designer clothing, cars, motorcycles and boats, shoes, hats, video games, computers, music, headphones, cologne, excessive male grooming. There is much blogging on the Internet of he said/she said about who is more materialistic: men or women. Regardless of sex, both are just as susceptible to a worldly life.

Materialism includes more than wealth. When we think about materialistic people, we often think of the wealthy and the stereotypical "rich kids" and you will find mostly spoiled brats like the "Rich Kids of Instagram", a Tumblr blog of photos from Instagram of young Americans showing off how they are enjoying the vast wealth of their parents and their possessions and experiences. They are materialistic no doubt, but research suggests that it is those who grew up in an environment of economic hardship who end up being more materialistic. The explanation is quite simple: those who grew up with whatever they never wanted to develop a passion for what they would want to, but cannot, have.

Chapter Key Takeaways

Find one's joy in life through God.

Choose to be content with what one has.

Invest in relationships

Focus on accumulating experiences and not things.

Limit television and skip the ads.

Give up magazines and catalogs for books.

Do not go to the mall or shopping for entertainment.

Monitor one's urges. Use a 30-day rule. When the 30 days have passed, if one still wants it, then consider whether it is needed.

De-clutter.

God wants one to value, desire and worship one and one thing only: Him.

The Church has a responsibility to provide life-stage lessons to assist with this life process.

Religious Health Eternity

*"My home is in heaven.
I am just traveling through this world."*
—Billy Graham

In this chapter, we share the opportunity to invest in eternity during this life and the spiritual needs of dying. Salvation is the most crucial lesson in this book.

Spirituality can be the search for a personal sense of life's meaning, value and purpose. Spiritual wellness, then, is the ability to create a sense of personal meaning in relationship to life's experiences, validate one's values in the face of life's uncertainties, and define a feeling of purpose for one's life.

Do not confuse spirituality with religion, says Rabbi Sara Paasche-Orlow of Hebrew Rehabilitation Center. Religious faith, practice, and involvement are merely one of many pathways to finding spiritual well-being in life. Rabbi Sara suggests the following tips for helping to maintain spiritual meaning in one's life:

Reach out to one's roommate, neighbors, tablemates, friends, and family for friendship and community.

Help make life better for others by offering help with a smile when seeing someone. If one enjoys religious community and practice, continue to attend services and stay involved.

Make time for rituals or prayers that are meaningful to one.

Share stories about one's life and experiences with like-minded people.

Continue to enjoy hobbies and activities that give pleasure.

Accept encouragement and praise from others, and offer the same.

Focus on the now and what each day can hold.

Learn something new every day.

Salvation

Salvation is a well-worn Christian term. We think we know what it means. However, biblically speaking, salvation is one of those significant terms that encircle several others, each of them reflecting a stunning facet of God's grace in Jesus Christ.

As a Christian, believe salvation requires:

Belief & Faith

Repentance

Confession

Baptism

By taking these steps by the Grace of the Father, Son, and the Holy Spirit, we receive the gifts of the Holy Spirit while on Earth until human death, and while in Heaven, spiritual life for eternity.

Life Stages Lessons is about both human and spiritual life, the now and the hereafter. With the stock market so uncertain, no other investment pays a better return, the Holy Spirit and Eternity.

However, salvation is only the first step. Jason Carter, Pastor of Worship Ministries of Village Church of Gurnee, Illinois, suggests there are seven additional responsible actions while on earth:

Pray

Read and know the Bible

Worship

Stewardship

Serve (Minister)

Witness (Evangelize)

Fellowship (identification with the body)

Do not divorce, cohabitate, watch pornography, continue with any other addictive habits

The fact is that God gave us thirty more years of life for a reason. In my opinion, elderhood is meant to lead us to accomplish the following:

The Ten Commandments
Exodus 20:1-17 (NIV)

Trust in God Commandment
Psalms 118.8 (NKJV)

The Sermon on the Mount
Matthew 5-7 (NIV)

The Building of His Church Commission
Matthew 16:18 (NIV)

The Great Commandment
Matthew 22:37-40 (NIV)

The Great Commission

Matthew 28:19-20 (NIV)

The Sermon on the Plain
Luke 6:17-49 (NKJV)

The Longevity Response-Ability
Commission John 3:16 (NIV)

The Stewardship Commandment
Colossians 3:23–24 (NIV)

Rejoice & Give Thanks Commandment
1 Thessalonians 5:16-18

Also, help with the following urgent issues:

Adult wellness and caring:

Communication

Fall prevention

Mental issues

Nutritional issues

Physical issues

Sexuality issues

Sleep issues

Social issues

Spiritual issues

AD and other dementia

Cultivation of an intergenerational culture

Death and dying preparation

Effective disciple-making

Establishment of a system to have meaningful contact with those leaving full-time employment and six months after that

Evangelism to the unchurched

Grandparenting

Helping oneself and others finish extremely well

Individual lay ministry leader philosophy

New beginnings and positive longevity attitude nurturing

Practicing stewardship and service:

A benevolent and generous lifestyle

Volunteering and working alongside gifted pastors

Longevity Response-Ability Crusade

Fundamental Retirement/Protirement Planning

USA Mission Harvest Campaign

Second Half of Life Ministry Seminary Curricula

Second Half of Life Prayer and Commitment

Sunday Flags Day

Prayer Corner

The above opportunities to serve are only the tip of the iceberg for investment in eternity

Joe's Story

The story is by Erica, his wife, as told to Wes & Judy Wick, Co-Founders of YES! Youth Enough to Serve. The story of Joe Capri shared in part (For the complete article see www.yestoserve.org/) reinforces what a blessing we can be when we move beyond a complacency mode and unleash the power of our elderhood protirement in the Lord's service.

When Joe was 70, an evangelist told him, "Joe, the Lord has impressed on my heart that you have made an idol of television and football. Moreover, if one is unwilling to get out of one's recliner and serve Him, He will take you home." On the Monday morning following this weekend encounter, Joe placed a call to a friend who served at the Spokane County jail. He asked if he could become a volunteer through the chaplain's office. They assured him that there was both a need and an open door. He went through preliminary training and began serving. As he continued to help, he pursued his ministerial credentials and eventually became the assistant chaplain at the jail, going there faithfully five days a week.

The inmates loved Joe's sincerity, discernment, and direct approach. One after another, God used Joe to help turn men's & female hearts to Christ. Early on he prayed he would live long enough for a thousand souls to turn to Jesus. Joe kept a running log of names. When the total number of salvation reached a thousand, he asked the Lord for another thousand.

At the age of 88, Joe had a stroke and put him in a wheelchair. With the assistance of friends, he continued visiting the jail for another two years, always looking for opportunities to lead others to Christ.

After his passing in May 2013, the chaplains and Erica reviewed Joe's monthly logs, which listed by name and date the men and women Joe was privileged to lead to Christ. A final tally found JUST OVER TEN THOUSAND names documented during Joe's twenty years of jail ministry, from age seventy to ninety!

As Erica pushed through the pain of grief in losing a best friend, she knows there are more lives to touch with the redeeming power of Jesus. His redemption can bring eternal life, breakthrough addiction, mend broken hearts, restore marriages, light a fire under complacent Christians, and touch the most incorrigible of criminals.

Now in the ninth decade of life, she still wants to make a difference. Moreover, perhaps by hearing Joe's testimony, others will be inspired to break away from the TV or from whatever else might hold one captive and step out in faith as a willing vessel of Christ.

Death and Dying

The second half of life includes both the fulfillment age (time of a more caring life) and the completion age (time of integration: polishing off, coming to terms with life, acceptance of eternity).

In the fulfillment age, one needs to complete three essential family needs: an estate plan, an executor document locator and a funeral plan.

The completion age is the least understood and most feared, because of our reluctance to think about death (discuss, pray or study what the Bible reassures).

As knowledge of the issues of death and dying increases, and positive attitudes promote, support of giving care will improve. It is vital to help the dying person through the transition that leads to the ultimate peaceful moment of death.

In 1993, K. J. Doka identified three spiritual needs of the dying:

Search for the Meaning of Life

To die appropriately

Hope that extends beyond the grave

The search for the meaning of life is different for everyone. Personally, the ISM for this life is that it is all about Him and investing in eternity.

In 2009, B. M. Dossey and L. Keegan identified appropriate dying factors to help the person pass to a peaceful death:

Gather family and friends

Keeping vigil at the dying person's bed

Touch

Hold

Talk

Reassure them of the hope and faith that extends beyond the grave

Continue to communicate with family and other caregivers supporting the dying person

Shut the half-closed eyes of the dying person, hug and stroke the physical body, and adjust the head on the pillow for the last time.

Chapter Key Takeaways

Complete one's salvation

Discovering His plan by following scriptures outlined below:

The Ten Commandments
Exodus 20:1-17 (NIV)

Trust in God Commandment
Psalms 118.8 (NKJV)

The Sermon on the Mount
Matthew 5-7 (NIV)

The Building of His Church Commission
Matthew 16:18 (NIV)

The Great Commandment
Matthew 22:37-40 (NIV)

The Great Commission
Matthew 28:19-20 (NIV)

The Sermon on the Plain
Luke 6:17-49 (NKJV)

The Longevity Response-Ability
Commission John 3:16 (NIV)

The Stewardship Commandment
Colossians 3:23–24 (NIV)

Rejoice & Give Thanks Commandment
1 Thessalonians 5:16-18 (NIV)

Pray for His strength to bolster one's courage

Read and study the reassurances in the Bible

Let the family know one's desires in dying. By providing the family with a written plan, one will understand that the wishes will be respected. Also, a written plan helps the family with the healing process, and better prepare them for their own passing one day

Provide loved ones an estate plan, an executor document locator and a funeral plan.

The Church has a responsibility to provide life-stage lessons to assist with this vital life process.

"Remember that when you leave this earth, you can take nothing that you have received...but only what you have given."
—Francis of Assisi

Elderhood Protirement Life Guides

Set one's goals in FAITH by Rick Warren:

FOCUSED: It is specific, something measurable.

ATTAINABLE: It is possible and practical. Set goals that are accomplishable.

INDIVIDUAL: It is personal. Do not set goals for other people. Take ownership over one's goals.

TRACKABLE: Your goal needs a deadline on it. Without a date on it, it's not a goal.

HEARTFELT: Be passionate about one's goals or the goals will never be accomplished.

The following are only for illustrative purposes:

Aging Reading Certification Series

Longevity Response-Ability Crusade

USA Mission Harvest Campaign

Second Half of Life Prayer and Commitment

Sunday Flags Day

Prayer Corner

Plan now (Redefine and refine continually)

You are Responsible

It is the Lord Jesus Christ you work for

The Lord owns all things

Pray

Read and know the Bible

Worship

Stewardship

Serve (Minister)

Witness (Identification with Body)

Avoid divorce, cohabitation, pornography, or continuation with an addictive habit

Develop an attitude of gratitude

Have a can do (self-reliance), will do (determined) attitude

Thank God first thing in the morning and last thing in the evening

What others think about one is not one's business

Make peace with your past (forgive everyone)

Love heals everything

Do not compare yourself or judge others

Measure three times, cut once

You are in charge of your happiness

Do not worry

Smile

Give back

Have a pet

Drink lots of water

Brush and floss your teeth

Dispose of things

Avoid clutter

Do not smoke

Avoid alcohol in excess.

Be optimistic, laugh, feel, have fun, and smile

Stay married and connected with others

Do not cohabitate no matter the reason

Continue to learn and exercise your mind

Never retire. Develop a second-half purpose

Pray, study the Bible and attend religious services

Get up, get going, get outside, walk, move, and keep busy

Eat grains, veggies, fish, and an apple a day, and take two fiber capsules after age 50

Chapter Key Takeaway

God has given everyone on average a 30-year bonus to help restore the American Dream and preserve Christianity, the Constitution, the Bill of Rights, democracy, the free enterprise system for society, nation, and the world.

The Church has a responsibility to provide life-stage lessons to assist with this essential life process.

Elderhood & Protirement Education

Minimize Communi-Chaos

God has given us 30 additional years of life, on the average. I genuinely believe these years are to help us to implement His plan for us while on Earth.

To accomplish our elderhood protirement plan, our church leaders and we need some specific training to overcome some shortsightedness and gain the initiative:

Reasons for Lack of Knowledge

Reasons for the lack of aging ministry training momentum include:

Lack of unity by the forces of intergenerational ministry and second-half ministry.

Lack of a standard core curriculum at theological educational institutions responsive to issues that affect people in the second half of life

Lack of corporate church body creative vision priority, and equipping.

Youth orientation and ageism bias

Older adults already Christians

Reluctance to change.

Institutional pastoral model.

A "group think" by an elected leadership that only they know best for the congregation.

Lack of local congregation leadership regarding continuing education, equipping active adult volunteers, intergenerational culture development and profiling for Kingdom building

Lack of standards for online educational training in the areas of certification in aging ministry, gerontology & readings; conferences, meetings, & workshops; Christian blogs & websites; and professional resource directories.

Lack of church initiative to take a more active role in societal change and national welfare

Lack of research and project implementation funding.

Primary Reasons for Training

Primary church life stages include childhood, adolescence, and adulthood. The primary focus is on youth. Seminary core curriculum does not provide elderhood (life beyond adulthood) training, according to a young pastor. Missy Buchanan, an author, columnist, and speaker on issues of aging and faith reported the following:

> A thirty-six-year-old minister explained that nothing in seminary had really prepared him for dealing with the real-life challenges of an aging population. With half of his congregation fifty and older, he was mainly interested in reaching young people. Besides, he felt clueless about how to engage older adults. He found it difficult to relate to boomers who seemed to be caught up in their own world, and he dreaded ministry to seniors who were

struggling with chronic health issues, loss of mobility and a lack of purpose.

As I inquired about the young man's seminary experience, he told me that aging had only been addressed as a minor part of a pastoral care class he had taken. In his recollection, it totaled less than an hour of class time. He had received no specific training for ministry with older adults, including the frail elderly. It was not surprising that he felt woefully ill-equipped to help more former congregants deal with unique lifespan issues.

I decided to explore some seminaries, and few seminaries offer a class on aging. In each case, it was offered as an option, not as a part of the core curriculum. Most often, aging was a minor subtopic in a pastoral care class, usually tied to grief or end-of-life counseling. A few seminaries offered certifications for those who had a specific interest in aging, but none required a course that would help all seminarians who will face a diverse, aging population in their appointments.

I can't help but wonder if our ministers wouldn't be more effective in ministry and leadership if they had a better understanding of aging and late-life transitions, especially in a culture that values youth over age. Could our seminaries provide them practical insight into the unique needs of each older adult sub-group—from boomers to frail—so that they could better empower all older adults to lean forward in life and utilize their skills and experiences to serve others?

The following Stephen Sapp and Larry Minnix excerpts from Missy Buchanan's website further testify to the need for education for church leadership and training for second-halfers:

Stephen Sapp, chair of religious studies at the University of Miami in Coral Gables, Florida, and former chair of the governing council for the Forum on Religion, Spirituality, and Aging said:

"People in the United States don't like old people, and church folks are not particularly different. Despite decades of awareness of ageism and a strong emphasis on battling all other 'isms,' old people (with the exception of lawyers and politicians) remain the only identifiable group that is perfectly acceptable to disparage, ridicule and demean in 'polite company.'"

Dr. Sapp suggests that one reason our youth-obsessed culture has a distaste for old people is that old people on some level confront us with what awaits most of us as we age.

When it comes to church growth, Dr. Sapp rejects the idea that attracting young families is the only answer. He expresses disappointment about the church's slow response to the apparent demographic shift to an aging population. He points to statistics that indicate if churches did nothing but attract people 65 and older, there are enough in the pipeline from that age group to double church membership every five years for the next 40 years or so.

Dr. Sapp says the typical American attitude about aging frames the conversation as a competition between young and old, and he dismisses the idea that if the church is to maintain its appeal to younger people, it must neglect old people. Instead, he emphasizes that what's needed is the recognition that we are all aging together. It is one thing every human being shares. As the body of Christ, we should remember that we are all in this together, he adds. The church ought to be the one institution in our society that lets no one forgets that."

Larry Minnix is a graduate of Candler School of Theology, an ordained minister and CEO of Leading Age, an association of 6,000 not-for-profit organizations dedicated to making America a better place to grow old by focusing on advocacy, education and applied research. Larry says his faith fuels his passion for evangelism for "the least of these."

"When I first went to Washington, D.C., in 2001, I was fired up to help vulnerable, older adults," he says. "I set out to work with legislators and White House officials, providing them with ideas, information, and resources about the aging population. I had this notion that we could come and reason together. Now I see my role as more prophetic than I had ever imagined."

Minnix thinks there should be no political spin when it comes to discussing important issues of aging and human vulnerability. He believes, too, that the church should be more aggressive in the national dialogue and taking a stand on eldercare matters.

When asked what a local congregation can do immediately to make a difference, he points to parish nurses, support programs for Alzheimer and dementia patients and adult day care programs.

Minnix strongly encourages churches to have strategic planning sessions to ask, "What is the role of the church regarding vulnerable populations?" From this dialogue, churches should begin to determine how the resources of the church can be more effective.

Minnix adds that churches have a role in helping people rethink the idea of retirement. He views retirement as an antiquated term. Though people in their sixties may leave a career after a long tenure, many will seek new career paths, including part-time work. The church must lead the way in showing them how to contribute their skills and gifts in ministry.

We need more people who will advocate for the well-being of seniors. More people who will give their resources instead of lip service. More people who want to be more like Jesus.

Key Educational Areas

What Senior Pastors, elected leaders, and interested laypersons need to do is commit to learning about the aging process (body, mind, and spirit). The process needs to start with a prayer by the entire congregation for the Holy Spirit's help with time and resources for a threefold initiative obtain aging ministry, basic gerontology, and aging reading certification.

The Center of Christian Leadership School of Theology, Anderson University in Indiana offers an online (www.anderson.edu/sot/ccl/aging.html) Certification of Aging Ministry for about $450. The purpose of the Certification in Aging Ministries is to provide a place where church leaders can receive training in how to lead a proactive, developmental ministry to and with older adults. The focus is on how people involved in aging ministries through the local church can develop quality programming that seeks to add life to 50plus years and view second-halfers as individuals who can significantly add to the ongoing ministry of the church and God's Kingdom.

McHenry County College in Illinois offers an online (www.ed2go com/online-courses/ HTML) gerontology certificate for about $225. This certification in gerontology is relevant for clergy, adult children of aging parents, and any other individual currently working with or planning to work with second-halfers.

The Certificate in Gerontology consists of 11 courses: Introduction to Gerontology; Physiology of Aging; Mental Health and Aging;

Healthy Aging; Pain Assessment and Management in the Older Adult; Death and Dying; Sleep and Aging; The Older Woman; Elder Abuse; Aging and Disorders of Communication and Alzheimer's Disease: Mysteries and Possibilities.

New Beginnings offers a no charge Aging Reading Certification to understand the new "Life Stage" and ministry "to" and "among" and "by" and "with" second-halfers alongside gifted pastors at no charge.

Selection Aging Reading List:

Second Half Elderhood Protirement Ministry (Second Edition)

Longevity Response-Ability (Second Edition);

Making an Aging Difference (Second Edition)

A New Life Stage (Second Edition)

Life Stages Lessons (Second Edition);

The Essential for Second-Half Ministry (Second Edition)

Planning the Life God Wants

Daily Legacy Living

Chism's Isms

The Second Half of Life

God's Grand

Fundamental Retirement/Protirement Planning

The program is available on the New Beginnings (www.gonewbeginnings.org/) website.

In 2013, New Beginnings launched a national Longevity Response-Ability Crusade.

In 2014, New Beginnings launched a local USA Elderhood Protirement Missions Harvest Campaign in Lake and McHenry counties of Illinois, with a particular focus within the communities and beyond, the Lord willing. Also in 2014 Second Half of Life Prayer and Commitment, and Sunday Flags Day started.

New Beginnings has developed a tool chest for helping second-halfers make the most of the next phase of their life. The resources were developed through years of research, education and personal experience to overcome barriers to creating a new and better society. The guides follow:

Individual Aging Plan Guides

Early Life
Next Generation
Salvation
Marriage
Stewardship
    Budget
    Estate
    Legacy
Elderhood Protirement
Wellness
Finishing Extremely Well

Church Aging Guides

Church Health
Congregational Analysis

Aging and Development Ministry
Reading Certification Series

Conferences, Meetings, & Workshops

The following are just a few programs available:

Baby Boomers and Beyond Weekend Contact Amy Hanson, Author, Consultant, Speaker Email: amy@amyhanson.org; 402-305-7530

How to Harness the Passion in 50+ Adults Seminar/ Workshop Contact Charles Arn, President of Growth, Inc. Charles.Arn @ChurchGrowth.net; 800-844-9286

re-ignite (guiding leading-edge Boomers in discovering purpose and passion in life and ministry) Retreat/ Groups Contact Leona Bergstrom, ChurchHealth Director. leonabergstrom@chonline.org; 425-314-8138

Helpful Websites

50 Alive! (www.50alive.com/): Empowering Boomers and Beyond to be all that God wants them to be.

Christian Grandparenting Network (www.christiangrandparenting.net/): Spiritual Legacy Builders

Missionnext (missionnext.org/): Your Bridge to Global Impact

New Beginnings (www.gonewbeginnings.org/): Seeking, Sharing with, Serving All ages

For a complete list of second-half resource websites and directory, please refer to the Appendix.

Chapter Key Takeaways

Areas of possible ministry training:

Certification in Aging Ministries

Certification in Gerontology

Certification in Aging Readings

The Church has a responsibility to provide life-stage lessons to assist with this essential life process.

Elderhood & Protirement
Longevity Response-Ability Crusade

"Never be lacking in zeal, but keep your spiritual fervor, serving the Lord. Be joyful in hope,a patient in affliction, faithful in prayer," Romans 12:11–12 (NIV).

New Beginnings is an online educational website dedicated to helping second-halfers finish exceptionally well. Its biblical educational compass follows:

The Ten Commandments
Exodus 20:1-17 (NIV)

Trust in God Commandment
Psalms 118.8 (NKJV)

The Sermon on the Mount
Matthew 5-7 (NIV)

The Building of His Church Commission
Matthew 16:18 (NIV)

The Great Commandment
Matthew 22:37-40 (NIV)

The Great Commission
Matthew 28:19-20 (NIV)

The Sermon on the Plain
Luke 6:17-49 (NKJV)

The Longevity Response-Ability
Commission
John 3:16 (NIV)

The Stewardship Commandment
Colossians 3:23–24 (NIV).

Rejoice & Give Thanks Commandment
1 Thessalonians 5:16-18 (NIV).

In 2013, New Beginnings launched a Longevity Response-Ability Crusade. The reform movement includes organizational, organized and individual strategic activities to grow God's love, joy, peace, patience, kindness, goodness, faithfulness, gentleness, and self-control as presented in Galatians 5:22-23 (NIV) to help the reader discover God's plan and carry it out to create a better second half of life society.

Organizationally, New Beginnings formed the Longevity Response-Ability Think Tank, affectionately referred to as Second Half of Life Visionaries. Sixteen members voluntarily wrote an Elderhood Directional Guide, entitled *Longevity Response-Ability*.

The book is responsive to current topics trending in the news. The theme of the book is doing what is possible, where one is, with what one has.

Longevity Response-Ability is a collection of readings (legacy letters, stories, and plans) written about what church leaders and second-halfers can do to unleash the determination and power of a new "life stage." The "tipping point" strategy follows: step one is to educate theological educational institutions, corporate church bodies, local congregations, nonprofit and private enterprises and governmental legislative bodies about the reality of a new "life stage." The second step is to educate those in the second half of life to their choices for making a difference. Achievement of this societal change requires a diverse ecosystem of both people and institutions working together.

Chapter Key Takeaway

Longevity Response-Ability was written to provide information, create awareness, provide momentum, and attract others to make social change.

The Church has a responsibility to provide life-stage lessons to assist with this crucial life process.

Elderhood & Protirement
USA Mission Harvest Campaign

We are the Planters & Waterers of His Word

New Beginnings has made a commitment to USA Missions Harvest Campaign in Lake and McHenry counties, with a particular focus within the communities of Gurnee, Lake Villa/ Lindenhurst, and Grayslake, the Lord willing.

The Go Initiatives are working examples of building His Church with love and by everyday life discipleship and evangelism in one's areas of influence and relationship clusters: Gender, Generation, Friends, Family, Interests/ Recreation, Need, Concerns/Problems, and Ethnicity/Culture. New Beginnings wishes to target all generations with an emphasis on all second-halfers and a particular focus on a new life stage, elderhood, the next stage after adulthood.

The Body of Christ is an interdependent body. God's family is intergenerational, and our God is an intergenerational God. Intergenerational and second-half ministries are complimentary. A key second-half ministry element is the development of intergenerational relationships and services.

The second-half ministry is not selfish; preferably it is the positive ripple effect of spiritually passionate, engaged older adults---within their families, their congregation family, and their community cluster families, according to Wes Wick.

Second-halfers are searching for answers. They are on a journey to balance their discretionary time with what is essential and what is satisfying. They are healthy, wealthy and mature. They are incensed with being marginalized. They are determined to improve our society.

Volunteer recruitment, training, and placement create a spiritual growth opportunity for using second-halfers' maturity to benefit the church, while they experience the joy of serving.

There are approximately 60 million second-halfers that need equipping to evangelize the other 82 million. Eighty-two million is the largest domestic missionary field in the history of our nation. The Great Commandment (Matthew 28:19-20) is closer than you may have realized.

The first step is the education of the societal hierarchy (every religious, educational institution, corporate church body, local congregation, nonprofit and private enterprise and governmental legislative body about the reality of a new "life stage"). Education should include:

Providing gerontological education to clergy in seminaries and training to existing religious staff

Creating programs that include home visits to older adults within the church family

Developing outreach and visitation programs to homebound elderly

Providing telephone reassurance programs

206

Providing devotional readings

Televising religious services

Creating prayer circles

Helping the search for personal meaning in life

Encouraging second-halfers to write their life story

Organize gifted volunteers working alongside gifted pastors together on second-half ministry ("to" and "among" and "by" and "with")

Addition of second-halfer services and expansion of small-group relationship-building opportunities with the unchurched to address issues that affect people in the second half of life:

Addictive behavior

Estate planning

Family budgeting

Benevolent and generous lifestyle

Grandparenting

Grief share

Legacy planning

Intergenerational mentoring, Latter life planning

Stewardship

Wellness Creation of new positions (volunteer, part-time, non-pastor):

Estate and planned-gift design
service

Development ministry

Church foundation

Aging and Development Ministry

Volunteer management (recruitment,
development, placement), and
Wellness

Establishment of a system to have
meaningful contact with those leaving
full-time employment and six months
after that

The second step is to educate those in the
second half of life to the choices of building a
better society:

Prepare for later life

Practice stewardship and service

Volunteer and work alongside gifted
pastors

Become a second-half unchurched
evangelist

Develop a benevolent and generous
lifestyle

Become an intergenerational mentor

Help others and self-finish extremely well

Chapter Key Takeaway

The USA Mission Harvest Campaign is an
invitation to equip 60 million second-halfers to
evangelize 82 million unchurched.

The Church has a responsibility to provide life-stage lessons to assist with this vital life process.

Elderhood Protirement
Service Opportunities

"Try not to become a man of success, but rather try to become a man of value,"
—Albert Einstein

Practicing stewardship and service:

A benevolent and generous lifestyle culture in stewardship, budget, estate, and legacy planning,

Aging Reading Certification Series

Fundamental Retirement/Protirement Planning

USA Mission Harvest Campaign

Second Half of Life Ministry Seminary Curricula

Second Half of Life Prayer and Commitment

Sunday Flags Day

Prayer Corner

Creation of an estate and planned-gift design service, as well as a church foundation for facility maintenance, renovation, and expansion

Early second-half preparation

Volunteer management: Recruitment, Development, and Placement

Individual lay ministry leadership philosophy

Volunteering and working alongside gifted pastors

Cultivation of an intergenerational 'We-Serve' Culture,

Establishment of a system to have meaningful contact with those leaving full-time employment (age 67 approximately) and six months after that

New beginnings and positive longevity attitude nurturing

Grandparenting

Grief sharing

Military family support

Adult wellness and caring: Communication, fall prevention, mental issues, nutritional issues, physical issues, sexuality issues, sleep issues, social issues, and spiritual issues

Helping oneself and others finish extremely well

Death and dying preparation

Chapter Key Takeaway

Do what one can, where one is, with what one has.

The Church has a responsibility to provide life-stage lessons to assist with this vital life process.

Epilogue

"I can do everything through Him who gives me strength,"
Philippians 4:10-12 (NIV).

A protirement elderhood life course plan needs to be in place when one or more of the following occurs:

Children graduate from college

Grandchildren begin to arrive

Family members move on to Eternity

Graduation from a public career

50th graduations celebrations

50th-anniversary celebration

The goal has been and continues to be & Protirement Financial, Spiritual, Physical, and Mental Health, plus Elderhood.

We covered several topics:

Stewardship

Estate

Legacy

Eternity

Mental Maintenance

Disease Prevention

Exercise

Nutrition

Frailty

Ageism

Entitlement

Materialism

Eternity

Life Guides

Education

Longevity Response-Ability Crusade

USA Harvest Mission Campaign

Service Opportunities

Knowledge is highly overrated without motivated hearts to implement the plan. His plan began before humans were born. By belief & faith, repentance, confession, and baptism, the Holy Spirit has been working from within one to achieve one's plan for Him. The Holy Spirit's identity is the activities He engages:

Brings Assurance

Convicts of Sin

Brings Understanding

Guides into Truth

Brings Comfort

Exalts Christ

Reveals God's Will

Calls into Service

Protects from Sin

Knows the Future

Produces Fruit

Places Members in the Body

Produces Unity

Gives Works

Reminds Us

May we all be "Doers," as defined by Pastor Rick Warren: "Doers love God with their strength. They are the energetic activists of life — the achievers, the accomplishers, the worker, and the people that push things forward and make things happen in the practical sense of life. The world needs contribution. We do not just need communication, compassion, and consideration. We have got to get to work and do it! We need people of action. We need people with initiative, energy, action, and a bias for achievement...when one becomes a believer, one's past disappears, one has a reason for living, and one has a home in Heaven...your personality does not change. God does not slow one down when one comes to Him. He changes one's direction. He wants to empower. Remember, one's personality is from Him. God does not want to make one a clone of everybody else in the way that one worship and serve and love Him. He wants one to serve Him with one's personality. Not only that, but He will strengthen one's personality, not dampen it. God is going to make one better than ever been before."

Chapter Key Takeaway
Pray to discover God's plan and use one's elderhood protirement years for Him.

The Church has a responsibility to provide life-stage lessons to assist with this vital life process.

About the Author

Life Stages Lessons is dedicated to elderhood, protirement, all ages, patriots planning, adjusting, and working their plan; my God, wife, family, friends, and teachers.

Those listed in the Professional Resource Directory herein were positive and supportive. Also, meaningful intellectual information excepts from Erica Capri, Milton Crum, Dave Ramsey; Larry Burke (deceased); Fidelity Investment; the Gray Panthers; Pastor Bruce Goettsche; Pastor Dr. Tim Smith; Jennifer Davis; Chauncey Crandall, M.D., and Gerontology Certification course material.

Robert W. Chism (Bob) is Certified in Aging Ministries (CAM) by the Center of Christian Leadership, School of Theology, Anderson University in Indiana, Gerontology, and Aging Readings; recognized for his second half of life research; founder of New Beginnings (www. gonewbeginnings.org/); an author, speaker; and consultant on second-half & intergenerational ministry training & equipping tools that Bob has been instrumental in developing.

Aging Resource
New Beginnings Website

Seeking, Sharing-with, Serving All Ages

New Beginnings is an online state of the art educational resource center website providing information, creating awareness and second-half social change by all generations.

Its action plan is to research, write, teach, speak, and consult on the second half of life for better understanding.

Its mission is to help all second-halfers finish exceptionally well.

Its goal is to help create awareness of a new life stage (age sixty-five to eighty-four), elderhood (life after adulthood). We are all in this together, growing older.

Its credo is as follows:

To differentiate a new life stage, elderhood

To age equality for the old and young

To encourage early discernment, planning, preparation of God's life plan, including protirement

To emphasize individuals of all age's ministry ("to" and "among" and "by" and "with") working together alongside gifted pastors

To focus on intentional all age evangelism

To coordinate volunteer church philanthropy

To pursue a generational, elderhood protirement, volunteer church staff, generosity, and aging and development ministry seminary curricula

New Beginnings has developed a tool chest for helping second-halfers make the most of the next phase of their life. The resources were developed through years of research, education and personal experience to overcome barriers to creating a new and better society. The guides follow:

Individual Aging Plan Guides

Next Generation
Salvation
Marriage
Stewardship
    Budget
    Estate
    Legacy
Elderhood Protirement
Wellness
Finishing Extremely Well

Church Aging Plan Guides

Church Health
Congregational Analysis
Aging and Development Ministry
Reading Certification Series

These guides are available in *Making an Aging Difference*.

New Beginnings books were written as seminary texts for training and equipping students; for seminary, graduate pastors; and elderhood protirement non-specialists desiring training and equipping for second-half evangelism and for the best use of their time for the Lord.

The goal is to help minister and train 142 Million second-halfers: 82 Million who need to God and 60 Million who need educating. 82 Million is the largest domestic missionary field in the history of our nation.

New Beginnings has published following books authored by Robert W. Chism:

Answers for the Next Generation is a guide to help equip, energize, and enable each generation insight into the appropriate solutions.

Life's questions just come, but the answers are difficult and innocuous

The book provides the facts about responsibility, salvation, stewardship, legacy, wellness, patriotism, age equality, elderhood & protirement understanding, and generation cognizance to one's life on earth and for eternity.

Second of Life Ministry Seminary Curricula was written to emphasize the need for Second Half of Life Ministry Seminary Curricula texts for training and equipping students; for seminary graduate pastors; and elderhood protirement non-specialists desiring education for the best uses their time for the Lord.

It also showcases an Aging Reading Certification Series.

The books were also written for a 12 Volume Aging Reading Certification Series and for young adults in planning their retirement/ protirement to finish extremely well.

12 Volume Aging Reading Certification Series

Fundamental Retirement/Protirement Planning is the 12th Volume for an Aging Reading Certification Series; for seminary text for training and equipping students, for seminary, graduate pastors, and elderhood protirement laymen desiring education second-half evangelism and the best use their time for the Lord; and for young adults in planning their retirement/ protirement to finish extremely well.

The God's Grand Plan focuses on the daily living characteristics of Jesus Christ: love, joy, peace, patience, kindness, goodness, faithfulness, gentleness, and self-control as found in Galatians," 5:22-23 (NIV).

To be happy for the rest of life, let Jesus's thoughts become thoughts and bend to His will.

Take charge of happiness. Believe and achieve!

The Second Half of Life is self-help for second-halfers to age happily and finished exceptionally well.

Chism's Isms is a collection of articles and essays for church leadership and second-halfers to grow, connect, serve, reach, and better prepare for a fuller, more productive, rewarding life and eternity with our Lord and Savior, Jesus Christ.

Daily Legacy Living is about starting a legacy plan at an early age if it is going to happen. Legacy is anything handed down from one generation to the next. It can be heredity, inheritance, or heritage. A legacy also leaves behind the story of a person, so that they are not forgotten. Legacies are important pathways for the future to follow or to be guided by to make better decisions in life. Leaving behind a legacy gives us comfort in knowing that once we are gone, in the memories of others. How one is remembered all depends on the person's actions.

Planning the Life God Wants was written for Christians, non-Christians, those in debt, those planning their life and those wishing to leave a legacy. The focus is on salvation and stewardship with a brief mention of mental and physical health. In our Christian walk, there is much to be accomplished in our congregation, community, state, and nation by fighting against the unshakable facts (challenge aging intolerance and conflict; unconstitutional government; and reclaiming our land as Christian and free).

The Essential Ingredients for Second-Half Ministry was written to answer the question as to the missing ingredients for the church to be successful with the new life stage of Elderhood, graduation from the public sector, and the protirement lifestyle.

Life Stages Lessons was written as an Alpha Tau Omega Life Guide for American's financial, mental, physical and religious health. Everyone, particularly children, grandkid, women, and elderhood adults, will benefit from the book. Life Stages Lessons focus on the matters that make a difference (Stewardship) in this life and make all the difference (Salvation) for eternity.

New Life Stage is about WHY God has provided us with an extra 30 years to make an eternal difference in our second half of life. The book teaches about a new life stage, elderhood, life after adulthood, and equips, energizes, and enables the new life stage, elderhood

Making an Aging Difference is a toolkit of guides for helping second-halfers make the most of the next phase of their life. Each chapter provides both information and instruction for helping to create a more productive second half of life and potential aging legacy.

Longevity Response-Ability is a collection of readings (legacy letters, stories, and plans) to help second-halfers grow, connect, serve, reach, and better prepare for a fuller, more productive, rewarding life and eternity with our Lord and Savior, Jesus Christ. See Book

Second-Half Elderhood Protirement Ministry (New Title, New Cover & Second Edition) is a thoroughly researched resource manual packed with relevant information and advice from proven sources.

All New Beginning's book royalties, after expenses, are contributed to funding research and free services

Aging Resource
Aging & Development Ministry

Unleashing All Ages Creativity & Power

The most compelling reason for second-half ministry (Elderhood Protirement) is that God has a purpose and plan for everyone (John 3:16). Elderhood is a documented life stage receptive to evangelism. Church growth author, teacher, and researcher Charles Arn identifies further reasons second halfers are receptive to conversion as closer to eternity, touch points, life changes and sweet spots (a sweet spot is one's God-given passion, motivator, stimulus, heartbeat, and gift).

"We are seeing indications that the Boomers may become more interested in spiritual matters in general, and Christianity specifically. The Baby Boomers have tried it all and found no joy. They may likely turn to the hope of the gospel," according to LifeWay Christian Resources.

The sample draft of the Second-Half (Elderhood Protirement) Aging and Development Ministry position follows:

AGING MINISTRY: Implement and direct a full-scale ministry to the whole person for the entire life by providing leadership, training, and mobilization opportunities:

For initial guidance, complete congregational research.

Facilitate the involvement of adult volunteer ministry with office space, desk, telephone, computer, business cards, web page, and newsletter.

Provide and coordinate a wide variety of ministry opportunities and activities to encourage meaningful involvement, spiritual growth, and facilitate the nurturing of relationships with members, non-members, and each generation.

Foster an intergenerational culture by integrating active adults with other "life-stages."

Provide life-stage support for issues significant to this segment of the congregation, such as life planning, health issues, aging with grace, aging parents' care, grandparenting, et al.

Develop, implement, and oversee coordinated in reach and outreach assimilation for second-halfers.

Provide training that will unleash/mobilize active adults to discover and use their gifts.

Create partnerships with agencies/organizations outside the church that dovetail with the second half ministry focus.

Develop budgets for the ministry consistent with youth ministry investment.

DEVELOPMENT MINISTRY: Identity, cultivate, and challenge partners; increase the level of generosity, participation, and ownership, through direct involvement and consistent financial giving:

Provide necessary leadership to initiate and implement a Church Estate and Planned-Gift Design Service, Foundation and development plan, to identify, cultivate, and challenge givers who have the potential to support the ongoing vision.

Provide leadership to Planned Giving efforts that would include education, marketing, presentations, proposals, gift arrangements, and gift closure.

Oversee the Foundation, work with the Foundation board to raise support for and help provide leadership to the Foundation.

Assure that gift arrangement is correctly completed and maintain an ongoing commitment to givers, building generosity into their lives.

Plan and carry out special dinners, events, and stewardship training that will maximize partnership with and raise financial resources for all ministries.

Maintain regular communication with the pastoral team to assure effective administration and prompt response to each giver's questions, concerns, and interests.

Take leadership to resource the organization's development plan further; educate and support each leader concerning his or her development and ministry role.

QUALIFICATIONS: Strong personal relationship with Jesus Christ as evidenced by spiritual maturity and a close daily walk with Him, consistent with the area of ministry and vision:

Be committed to the theological stance of the church.

Possess an understanding of the ministries of the church.

Proven knowledge, experience, and success in not-for-profit development

College degree in business communications, marketing, or related discipline

Advanced development, aging training, and personal research are highly desirable.

Working with Church Staff and Volunteer

RELATIONSHIPS:

Reports directly to the senior pastor.

Develop and be responsible for departmental meetings, staff, and volunteers, as needed.

Be informed of and function within the guidelines outlined in the church bylaws.

FIVE YEAR POSITION DELIVERABLES:
Intergenerational Ministry Culture
Intentional Second-Half Adult Evangelism
Benevolence and Generosity Development
Church Estate and Planned Gift Design
Service Church Foundation

The position incorporates concepts from "Job Description about Older Adults", by Amy Hanson; EFCA Encore Sample Job Description Resources,by Chris Holck; "What This Baby Boomer SeniorPastor Learned at a CASA Network ITC", by Joe Boerman, Senior Pastor, Immanuel Church, Gurnee, IL; and networking

with Charles Arn, Church Growth, Inc.,
Monrovia, CA.

Aging Resource
Website List

AARP (www.aarp.org) is a nonprofit membership organization of persons 50 and older dedicated to addressing their needs and interests. It has more than 39 million members, and its aims include informing members and the public on issues important to this age group, advocating on legislative, consumer and legal issues, promoting community service, and offering a wide range of unique products and services to members.

Aging Services of California (www.aging.org) is the leading advocate for quality nonprofit senior living and care in the state. This public-interest association represents more than 400 nonprofit providers of aging services (including affordable housing, continuing care retirement communities, assisted living, skilled nursing, and home and community-based care) that collectively serve more than 100,000 older adults. The association also directs a statewide public education campaign – "Aging is an Active Verb."

The American Federation for Aging Research (www.infoaging.org) provides the latest research-based information on a wide range of age-related diseases, conditions and issues.

America Society on Aging (www.asaging.org) is the largest organization of multidisciplinary professionals in the field of aging. Its resources, publications, and educational opportunities are geared to enhance the knowledge and skills of people working with older adults and their families.

Center Sage (www.gbod.org/minister-to-people/center-sage) is a newsletter published quarterly by The General Board of Discipleship (GBOD), an agency of The United Methodist Church.

Civic Ventures (www.civicventures.org) engages millions of boomers in the workforce. Founded in 1998, the organization's programs, original research, and strategic alliances demonstrate the value of people's experience in solving pressing social problems. Its national service program, Experience Corps (www.experiencecorps.org), works with more than 2,000 members in 20 cities to help 20,000 students.

Gerontological Society of America (www.geron.org) is the nation's oldest and largest multidisciplinary organization devoted to research, education, and practice in the field of aging. The primary purpose of the Society – and its 5,200-plus members – is to advance the study of aging and disseminate information among scientists, decision makers, and the general public.

International Longevity Center – USA (www.ilcusa.org), founded in 1990 by world-renowned gerontologist and Pulitzer Prize-winning author Robert N. Butler, M.D., is the first nonprofit, nonpartisan, international research, policy and education organization formed to educate individuals on how to live longer and better, and advise society on how to maximize the benefits of today's age boom.

New Beginnings (www.gonewbeginnings.net/) is a website for those in the second half of life and dedicated to seeking, sharing with, and serving all ages.

The OASIS Institute (www.oasisnet.org) is a national, nonprofit educational organization designed to enrich the quality of life for mature adults. Seeking to keep older people active in the community through educational and volunteering programs, OASIS offers programs such as Positive Attitudes and Positive Aging to help people deal with the stresses of aging.

POAMN Network News (www.poamn.org/index.php/newsletter) is a newsletter published quarterly by the Presbyterian Older Adult Ministries Network, an affiliation of the Presbyterian Church (USA).

Stanford Center on Longevity (http://longevity.stanford.edu) has a mission to transform the culture of aging by combining scientific and technological discoveries with swift entrepreneurial action. The SCL links top scholars with the government, business and improving memory, and using technology to enhance savings and healthcare.

Third Age (www.thirdage.com) is a vibrant online resource for older people, with articles on issues relevant to people over 40 and to those who want to build a genuine relationship with older people, such as relationships, romance, health, wellness, well-being, spirituality, and personal growth and development.

University of Pittsburgh's "Generations Together: An Intergenerational Studies Program" (www.gt.pitt.edu) focuses on intergenerational relationships and taps the wisdom of age, with programs such as the Intergenerational Early Childhood Program, Youth in Service to Elders, and Intergenerational Artist Education Program, which links older masters of the visual, literary and performing arts with budding artists.

Gerontology Program, the University of North Carolina at Greensboro (www.uncg.edu/gro), delivers leaders in the profession with the highest quality trans-disciplinary education in gerontology and performs necessary and applied research, preparing students for academic and professional careers serving age-related markets nationwide.

USC Davis School of Gerontology (www.usc.edu/dept/gero) is the nation's leader in the field of gerontology and has consistently pioneered innovative educational programs. Through the efforts of the faculty, staff, and Board of Councilors, the Andrus Gerontology Center is committed to promoting successful aging and an older population that is healthy, active and involved in the life of the community and nation.

Aging Resource
Professional Directory

Individuals listed alphabetically:

Charles Arn
President, Church Growth Inc.
Professor of Outreach and Ministry Wesley
Seminary and Author
www.churchgrowth.net/index.htm
ChipArn@aol.com

John Aukerman
Director Center for Christian Leadership
School of Theology at Anderson University
jhaukerman@anderson.edu
765-641-4530

Leona Bergstrom
Director Re-Ignite and Author
www.re-ignite.net/
leonaberg@comcast.net
206-362-2621

Missy Buchanan
Author, Columnist, and Speaker on issues of
aging and faith
missy@missybuchanan.com
417-642-5677

Robert W. Chism
Founder of New Beginnings, Researcher,
Author, Teacher, Speaker, Consultant
www.gonewbeginnings.org/
chism.w.robert@comcast.net
224-222-8900

Milton Crum
Old age octogenarian writer
2crums@bresnan.net

Peggy Fulghum
Director, Boomer Builder Ministries
Johnson Ferry Baptist Church
www.johnsonferry.org/laf.aspx
peggy.fulghum@jfbc.org
770-794-2975

David P. Gallagher
Speaker, Pastor, and Author
www.agingsuccessfullytoday.com/
drdavog@gmail.com
602-509-1732

Richard H. Gentzer, Jr
Executive Director ENCORE Ministry Gold
Cross Foundation of the Tennessee
Conference-UMC; the former Director of the
Center on Aging & Older Adults Ministries for
the General Board of Disciples; part of the
Adjunct Faculty for the School of Transform
Aging at Lipscomb University; an author and
coauthor of books and articles on aging and
older adult ministry
www.encoretnumc.org
Richard.gentzler@tnumc.com
615-479-6175

Amy Hanson
Author, Speaker, Consultant
www.amyhanson.org/
amy@amyhanson.org
402-305-7530

Cavin Harper
Executive Director
Christian Grandparenting Network
www.christiangrandparenting.net/
cavinharp@gmail.com
719- 522-1404

John Heide
U.S. Missionary to those in the Second half of Life, Author, and Speaker
50 ALIVE
www.50alive.com/
johnheide2002@yahoo.com
417-838-0059

Chris Holck
President, Encore Generation
Planter and Pastor of Live Oaks Community Church
www.encoregeneration.wordpress.com/
chrisholck@me.com
612-803-0881

Nelson Malwitz
Chief Innovation Officer, Missionnext
www.missionnext.org/
nelsonm@missionnext.org
203-733-3190

Richard Morgan
Recipient of the 2013 Legacy Award from the POAM of the Presbyterian, Church, USA, for his nineteen books, countless presentations, and elderhood work.
www.richardmorgandr.wordpress.com/
richardmorgan12921@comcast.net
724- 864-4205

Dave Ramsey
Creator of Financial Peace University (FPU) and Author
www.daveramsey.com/pr/bio/
info.general@daveramsey.com
888-227-3223

Chuck Stecker
President Center for Intergenerational Ministry
President/Founder A Chosen Generation
www.achosengeneration.org
chuck@achosengeneration.org
303-948-1112

Ward Tanneberg
Writer, Author, Speaker, Pastor Emeritus
http://www.wardtanneberg.com/
425-455-7599

Rick Warren
Pastor, Saddleback Church, Philanthropist,
and Author
www.saddleback.com/
info@saddleback.net
949- 609-8000

Wes and Judy Wick
Co-Founders of YES! Young Enough to
Server,
USA Missionaries for those in the Second Half
of Life
www.yestoserve.org/
wes@yestoserve.org/ judy@yestoserve.org
831-359-5308/ 831-359-1046

Aging Resource
Book Library

Alphabetically listed:
40 Days of Love (2008), Rick Warren
A Shepherd Looks at Psalm 23 (2007), W. Philip Keller
A New Life Stage (Second Edition) (2015), Robert W. Chism
Aging and Ministry in the 21st Century (2008), Richard Gentzler, Jr.
Aging Successfully (2012), David P. Gallagher
Aging Well Bible Study Series (2014), Pete Menconi
Aging, the Individual, and Society (2007) S.M. Hillier and G.M. Barrow
Amazing Grays (1999), Leona and Richard Bergstrom
An Age of Opportunity: Intentional Ministry by, with, and for Older Adults (2018), Richard Gentzler, Jr.
Answers for the Next Generation (2019), Robert W. Chism
Baby Boomers and Beyond (2010), Amy Hanson
Catch The Age Wave (1999), Win Arn and Charles Arn
Celebrating Disciples (1988), Richard Foster
Changing Course (2007), William A. Sadler
Chism's Isms (2014), Robert W. Chism
Concise Theology (2001), J.I. Packer
Daily Legacy Living (2014), Robert W. Chism
Encore (2007), Michael Kinsman
Encountering the New Testament (2005), Walter Elwell, Robert Yarbrough
Encountering the Old Testament (2008), Bill Arnold, Bryan Beyer

Faith is a Verb (2008, 1987), John Aukerman, David Neidert/ Ken Stokes

Faith Is a Verb: A Workbook (2008), John Aukerman

Financial Peace Revisited (2003), Dave Ramsey

Financial Peace University Workbook (2010), Dave Ramsey

Finishing Life Strong (2011), John Heide

Finishing Well (2011), John Dunlop, M.D.

Follow Your Calling (2012), John Bradley and Nelson Malwitz

Four Seasons of Leadership (2008), David Neidert

Fundamental Retirement/Protirement Planning (2015), Robert W. Chism

Generous Living (1997), Ron Blue

God's Grand Plan (2015), Robert W. Chism

God's Plan of Significance (2007), Jerry and Shirley Rose

Graying of the Church (2004), Richard Gentzer, Jr.

Heartbeat! (2011), Charles Arn

How to Finish the Christian Life: Following Jesus in the Second Half (2012), Donald W. Sweeting and George Sweeting

How to Minister Among Older Adults (2005), Charles Knippel

How to Retire (2011), Ernie Zelinski

How to Start a New Service (1997), Charles Arn

Irresistible Evangelism (2003), Sjogren, Ping, Pollock

Joy Boosters (2012), Missy Buchanan

Knowing God (1993), J.I. Packer

Living by the Book (2007), Howard Hendricks and William Hendricks

Life Stages Lessons (Second Edition) (2015), Robert W. Chism

Longevity Response-Ability (Second Edition) (2015), Robert W. Chism

Making an Aging Difference (Second Edition) (2015), Robert W. Chism

My Plan for Finishing Well (2014) Jim Carlson

Management Essentials for Christian Ministries (2003), Michael Anthony

Master Your Money (2004), Ron Blue

Maximize (2010), Nelson Searcy

My Plan for Finishing Well (2014) Jim Carlson

My Next Phase (2007), Eric Sunstrom

New Bible Dictionary (1996), Marshall, Millard, Packer, Wiseman

Older Americans, Vital Communities (2007), W. Andrew Achenbaum

One Church, Four Generations (2002), Gary L. McIntosh

Planning the Life God Wants (2014), Robert W. Chism

Second Half (2017), Wes Wick

Second-Half Elderhood Protirement Ministry (Second Edition) (2015), Robert W. Chism

Second Half of Life (2014), Robert W. Chism

Second Half of Life Ministry Seminary Curricula (Second Edition) (2019), Robert W. Chism

Senior Adult Ministry in the 21st Century (2002), David P. Gallagher

Significance (2010), R. Jack Hansen

Simply Strategic Volunteers (2005), Tony Morgan and Tim Stevens

Spirit Boosters (2016), Missy Buchanan

Super-Charged (2009), Mary Lloyd

The 8th Habit (2006), Stephen Covey

The Foundations of Leadership (2011), Gordon MacDonald

The Gift of Significance (2000), Doug Manning
The Intergenerational Church (2008), Peter Menconi
The Jesus Creed (2004), Scot McKnight
The Launch Bible study series (2011), EFCA Encore
The New Breed (2007), Jonathan and Thomas W. McKee
The Procrastinator's Guide (2007), Eric G. Matlin
The Purpose Driven Church (1995), Rick Warren
The Purpose Driven Life (2003), Rick Warren
The Essential Ingredients For Second-Half Ministry (Second Edition) (2015), Robert W. Chism
The Third Age (2000), William A. Sadler
The Third Calling (2016), Leona and Richard Bergstrom
The Treasure Principle (2001), Randy Alcorn
Theology in a Nutshell (2008), Ken Horn
Voices of Aging (2015, Missy Buchanan
White Unto Harvest (2003), Charles Arn
Working the Gray Zone (2000), Charles G. Oakes

www.ingramcontent.com/pod-product-compliance
Lightning Source LLC
Chambersburg PA
CBHW070951040426
42443CB00007B/458